Henry Beston's Cape Cod

The Story Behind a Gallant Vagabond's Search
for the Great Truth on Eastham's Outer Beach

By Don Wilding

*Merry Christmas
from Henry's Outer
Beach!*

D. Wilding

Copyright © 2003 by Donald A. Wilding

ISBN 0-7414-1359-0

Published by:

INFINITY
PUBLISHING.COM

519 West Lancaster Avenue
Haverford, PA 19041-1413
Info@buybooksontheweb.com
www.buybooksontheweb.com
Toll-free (877) BUY BOOK
Local Phone (610) 520-2500
Fax (610) 519-0261

Printed in the United States of America

Printed on Recycled Paper

Published January 2003

In Memory of Nan Turner Waldron
1922 – 2000

"In my mind's eye remains the mystery
and the wonder of it all
While the journey still lies ahead."

Foreword

My "journey" to *The Outermost House* began in 1996, when my wife, Nita, and I started taking short trips to the outer reaches of Cape Cod. This area, complete with rolling dunes, blue sea and a mystical aura about it, had always enchanted me, and now I had the opportunity to get to know it first hand.

One day, while visiting the Cape Cod National Seashore's Provincelands Visitors Center in Provincetown, Nita and I purchased two books – Henry David Thoreau's *Cape Cod*, and *The Outermost House* by Henry Beston. That evening, we chose our reading -- I took Thoreau, my wife took Beston. While Thoreau's book was wonderful, it didn't fill the void. "You're going to love this book," Nita said of *The Outermost House*. I haven't put it down since.

The Outermost House is now considered a classic of American Literature and has a small (compared with some other literary works) but devoted following. Beston (or "Henry," as he's referred to in the pages of this book) wrote *The Outermost House* after spending a solitary "year" in a 20x16-foot house on the dunes of Eastham, using the house as a base while studying and observing the wonders of the elements in this glorious maritime setting. Beston died in 1968, and the house was washed away nearly 10 years later. The spirit of Beston's work continued in the pages of *Journey to Outermost House* by Nan Turner Waldron in 1991.

"The little house is gone. Henry Beston and the high dunes of Nauset are gone, as all things eventually are in this temporal passage," Nan Waldron wrote. She went on to say that Beston's book "is about a setting

i

alive with the living ... It is less about either the place of the people and more of how Cape Cod makes you feel and what it does to you, and I would add 'for you,' because I believe that being close to the natural environment inspires a quest, perhaps inherent in Man, to understand human nature."

I was fortunate to meet Nan Turner Waldron in January 2000. It's pretty safe to say that no one spent as much time, or became a part of the Fo'castle (as Beston called the house) as she did. Nan Waldron is gone, having passed away on November 8, 2000, but her influence had a major impact on a 30-something sportswriter searching for a little bit more out of life.

Nan's battle with cancer had experienced many peaks and valleys over the previous two years. In September of 2000, she received news that there was nothing more that could be done about it. This revelation startled me, and throughout my visit with her, I found myself numb from the news. But as my visit with her was ending and she accompanied me to the door, she looked at me reassuredly, and smiled.

"I've accepted it, Don," she said. "There's nothing I can do about it. I'll be 79 years old in January, and I've had a wonderful life. It's OK."

Nan paused as she stood in the doorway and I on her porch, still dumbfounded, taking it all in. She smiled again and nodded. "It's OK."

Although I could only imagine what she was going through, I knew that she had been fighting hard, for so long. This woman, who had walked so many miles of the outer beach, who had climbed all 3,165 feet of New Hampshire's Mount Monadonock on Thanksgiving Day four years earlier, could not overcome this obstacle.

We all knew that her spirit was living on when she wrote that "in my mind's eye remains the mystery and the wonder of it all ... While the journey lies ahead."

* * * * * * * *

For the last five years, I've lived in a small apartment about 95 miles from Beston's beach, but that hasn't stopped me from making frequent trips to Coast Guard Beach in Eastham in all kinds of weather. Two days after meeting Nan Waldron, I walked Coast Guard Beach on a frigid January day, with wind chill factors reaching 40 degrees (F) below zero. Most people would say I'm nuts, but after that experience, I understood even more where Beston and Waldron were coming from. I began to look forward to the fall each year, knowing that a place that prompted Beston to write that "the beauty of this earth and outer sea so possessed and held me that I could not go," awaited me.

I was hooked.

While Beston's book is cherished by many, there are countless others who have never heard of it. Even in today's world, Beston's words still ring true. Here was a man who, tired of his work as an editor, still shaking from the horrors of World War I, and looking for his place in the literary world, found some peace in an otherwise mad world.

Today, so many more yearn to find this same kind of peace. His book is also considered one of the seminal works of today's environmental movements; even in the 1920s, he lamented over the devastating effects of oil slicks on the birds and other wildlife of the sea.

In September 1999, I established a Web site known as *The Outermost Web Site* at http://outermost.tripod.com . The site now comes up at or near the top of many search engines when you type in "Henry Beston" or "Outermost House." After meeting Nan Waldron, the site expanded as I learned more about the subject. A few months later, Nan told me about the town of Eastham's plans to host a 350th Anniversary celebration in 2001. A chance meeting with Cape Cod author Robert Finch, who wondered "I'm surprised that no one's ever done a biography on Beston," further fueled my quest. Contact with the Eastham 350 committee followed, and the 32-page magazine tribute to Beston and *The Outermost House*, titled *On its Solitary Dune*, was printed in January of 2001.

As part of Eastham's 350th Anniversary celebration, I was fortunate to present lectures in Eastham during the summer of 2001. Another lecture followed in Sandwich in early 2002. The project for this book began to take shape.

Meanwhile, many others from around the country and beyond were writing and calling, expressing enthusiasm for the renewed interest in Beston and his beloved "Fo'castle." "Nice work -- Beston needs to be better known," many of the notes and e-mails have read.

Henry Beston's Cape Cod is not a biography, but instead takes us on the journey undertaken by Beston in his quest for literary and spiritual peace of mind. Beston and *The Outermost House* have left a legacy; *Henry Beston's Cape Cod* tells the story of how that legacy came about.

In January of 2002, while I was writing this book, my wife and I began efforts to form The Henry

Beston Society, which aims "to honor Henry Beston by stimulating interest in and promoting education about his life, works and philosophy -- with emphasis on his time spent on Cape Cod in Massachusetts -- and his place in his world and ours, by coordinating research on his life and writings, by acting as an archive for material relevant to Henry Beston and by advocating for the preservation of the memory and historical importance of *The Outermost House*." More on The Henry Beston Society can be found online at www.henrybeston.org .

Henry Beston's Cape Cod would not have been possible without the efforts and encouragement of many people, not in any particular order: George Rongner; Beverly Plante; Don Sparrow; Marie Beston Sheahan; Ted Waldron, Lesley Waldron, the Waldron family and Butterfly & Wheel Publishing; George and Rosemary Abbott; Merton Stevens; Bill Quinn Sr.; Kate Alpert; Helen Mourton, Ed Harnett and Marilyn Schofield of The Eastham Historical Society; Bethany Rutledge and Jeanne Johnson of The Thornton W. Burgess Society, Sandwich, Mass.; Terry Ryan of The Patriot Ledger, Quincy, Mass.; Barbara Stamos of The Quincy Historical Society; Jeanine Thubauville of The Crane Public Library, Quincy, Mass.; Doug Capra; Fran Murphy Zauhar of St. Vincent's College, Latrobe, Penn.; Ian and Nan Aitchison; Marcia Nickerson; Bob Seay of WOMR-FM in Provincetown, Mass.; Conrad Nobili; Ray Brown of WCRB-FM in Boston; the Eastham 350th Anniversary Publications Committee; Walter Brooks and the staff of *Cape Cod Today* and *Best Read Guide*; Jeff Peterson, Frank Mortimer, Vin Igo, Jack Authelet and the staff of *The Foxboro Reporter* in Foxboro, Mass.; and the staff of *The Sun Chronicle* in Attleboro, Mass.

Jon and Kerrie March have been a source of inspiration and support since I first met them at the presentation of Ronald Perara's *The Outermost House* as part of the Eastham 350th Anniversary festivities at Nauset High School in Eastham. Credit also goes to Bill Quinn and Jon for coming up with the title for the book. May Jon (a.k.a. "Jonny Swing"), Kerrie and Cookie long roam the dunes of Nauset!

I also want to thank my family for their love and support – particularly my daughter, Amanda Wilding, and my son, Matthew Wilding. Also, a million thanks go to my parents, Vincent and Harriet Wilding. I'm grateful for the encouragement from my uncle and aunt, Gus and Anita Grossi; and very much obliged to my in-laws, Tom and Betty Galloway, for the use of their own "Outermost House" in Provincetown.

Finally, this project would never have been possible without the love and support of my wife, Nita, who also helped copy edit the manuscript. Nita has made this journey with me every step of the way, for which I am eternally grateful.

God bless and best regards,

Don Wilding

North Attleborough, Massachusetts
September 2002

HENRY BESTON'S CAPE COD

Contents

**The Fo'castle and its owner stand high on the dune overlooking the
Atlantic Ocean.**

(Photo courtesy Wheelwright Museum of the American Indian,
Santa Fe, NM)

I. The Fo'castle Rises on the Dunes

It was June of 1925 in the Cape Cod town of Eastham, and Henry Beston was traipsing through the dune land between the Atlantic Ocean and Nauset Marsh.

Cooped up for months behind the walls of New York City's Prince George Hotel, Henry, or "Henry B." as he often signed his name, was relieved to be out of the congestion of the big city and back breathing in the salt air of Eastham.

Most of the time that Henry made this walk down the beach, he was alone and not heading anywhere in particular. Usually, he'd walk along at a comfortable pace, taking in his surroundings. One of Henry's greatest talents was his keen sense of observation, and it was during these walks that he'd use this talent to the fullest.

Henry was wrapping up his fifth book, titled *The Book of Gallant Vagabonds.* "There are times when everyone wants to be a vagabond, and go down the road to adventure, strange peoples, the mountains, and the sea," he reasoned. "The bonds of convention, however, are many and strong, and only a few ever break them and go."

Henry was a vagabond -- a gallant one at that -- like never before. He described a "Gallant Vagabond" as being "the wayfarer with scarce a penny in his pocket who fights his way upstream to see where the river rises, and crosses the dark mountains to find the fabled town. His curiosity is never purely geographical, it lies in the whole fantastic mystery of life."

Henry was about to break those bonds of convention. He would literally rip them off and shred them to pieces.

This late spring day wasn't just any day. Today, Henry wasn't alone on his walk. A carpenter and his construction crew followed directly behind him. The crew dragged a hearty supply of lumber and bricks through the sand on the road that ran along the marsh, waiting to see where this giant of a man from the mainland wanted them to unload their cargo.

To the north of this magnificent stretch of sand was the Nauset Coast Guard Station. The dune land stretched out nearly three miles to the south and about a quarter of a mile from east to west. The marsh separated the dunes and the mainland. On the dunes, the only structures one might find would be a few gunning shacks or small cottages, many haphazardly built.

Finally, Henry scaled a dune that was only about 20 feet above the high water mark of the ocean side. The carpenters, not far behind, looked up, waiting for a signal.

"This is where I want it," Henry said to Harvey Moore, the head carpenter.

"It" was a sturdily-built house, 20 feet by 16 feet. Harvey and his crew -- which included future Eastham Police Chief and Selectman Winnie Knowles; Harvey's son, Horace; and Lenny Brewer, went to work building the structure that Henry wanted. He called this house "The Fo'castle" and it would sit on the dune facing the ocean like a ship at sea.

Henry had grown up in the seacoast town of Quincy, Massachusetts, and served as a naval correspondent aboard a U.S. Navy submarine less than a decade earlier during World War I. Throughout the war, he witnessed more than his share of horrific events. The thought of being alone in a solitary setting with the waves, the sand and the open sky, with the Fo'castle as a home base, was tremendously appealing.

Henry may not have known it at the time, but this house is what author Nan Turner Waldron would later refer to as his "spiritual chrysalis." This spot of sand is where Henry -- who had dropped his given surname of Sheahan only a few years earlier -- would find his place in literary history.

Eastham, Massachusetts was a village of open moorland known for the high quality turnips and asparagus that grew in its sandy soil. Many of its residents may have thought this newcomer from the mainland was a bit on the daffy side.

This, however, didn't phase the carpenters and the officers of the Coast Guard, who patrolled the outer beaches from their station two miles to the north. For Henry possessed an engaging personality and friendly disposition in his 6-foot, one-inch, 190-pound body, and had become like one of the family to some of Eastham's town folk. Many of them described Henry as "a breath of fresh salt air."

Henry stayed with a few families in the area of Eastham near the Salt Pond for the last couple of years, and Harvey Moore had been one of his neighbors. Henry himself drew up the plans for his house on the dunes, and Harvey, probably the only carpenter in town, was a natural choice to build it.

Harvey Moore, the Eastham carpenter who built the Fo'castle for Henry Beston in 1925.
(Photo courtesy Thornton W. Burgess Society, Sandwich, Mass.)

Harvey served as a constable in the town of Eastham for nearly three decades, holding that position until just before he died at the age of 90 in 1967. "He was a friendly fellow, good on ideas and explanations," Henry would say of Harvey many years later. Burton Kelley, who lived at the nearby Overlook Inn, described Harvey as "the most casual business man I ever saw. He never hurried and if he didn't have paint, nails or wood, which he needed, he would do something else or use something else until he could get it."

Harvey's crew took about four weeks to complete Henry's house, which drew many compliments on its location and appearance. Only a few months earlier, Henry sought advice from friends

4

as to whether he should stain the walls a shade of brown and apply a coat or two of blue paint to the furniture.

However, the chosen site prompted Captain Abbott Walker of the Coast Guard to issue a few words of caution to Henry. "It's a good place for it," Captain Walker said, "But it's a little too near high tide." Years later, Henry would admit, "Sure enough, it proved that way."

For the moment, though, Henry sensed he was close to the peace of mind that he'd been seeking for some time. He no longer had to deal with the horrors of war, or to slave away in an editor's office in New York City. He "had a little money," and was still a bachelor. His sole family obligations were to his mother, Marie, and older brother, George, a noted Quincy surgeon. He had traveled all over the world -- to England, France, Spain, Mexico -- and had also logged his share of miles within the borders of the United States.

Yet, none of this would impact his life the way this "Outermost of Lands" did.

"The house was very, very well built," Henry said many years later. "It was a sturdy house and everybody liked it. It was easy to keep clean and look after.

"I had only one rule -- it was always clean up the breakfast and make my bed and clean up the house, and then, after that, anything could happen."

Something would happen in this house that everybody liked, all right -- something almost mystical. It turns out that what Henry Beston would describe while experiencing life in this house was something that he -- along with millions of adoring readers around the world -- would cherish forever.

Henry Beston during World War I.

(Photo courtesy Marie Beston Sheahan)

II. The Road to Vagabondage

At the age of 37, Henry was about to find himself as a writer in friendly confines – by himself with only the open sky, open Atlantic and majestic dunes in his presence.

For many years, Henry expressed an eagerness to get back to the sea. He grew up in Quincy, Massachusetts, the son of a surgeon. He referred to his early years living on School Street as "a New England boyhood of sea and shore, enriched with a good deal of the French spirit, from a French mother." He always had, as he would write in the pages of *Full Speed Ahead*, an "early passion for the beauty and mystery of the sea."

Henry was born Henry Beston Sheahan on June 1, 1888, to Dr. Joseph Sheahan and Marie Louise (Maurice) Sheahan. Marie Sheahan, who was born in France, had a great influence on him and Henry learned to speak and write English and French equally well. His mother, who was of Parisian descent from a French military Bonapartist family, also introduced Henry to the theater, which would become one of his life's great passions. If there was anything that he loved more than the theater, it was the constellations of the stars – the theater of the natural world.

Dr. Joseph Sheahan was a general practitioner and often took young Henry with him on his rounds. On one of those rounds, Henry went to the Adams mansion (home of the early presidents) and met Henry Adams, a noted poet of the times.

Writer Elizabeth Coatsworth, who eventually became Mrs. Beston, once said, "Henry always had the magnetism that is an inborn gift, something over and above his voice, the clear cut of his mouth or the expression of his eyes, His father ... must have had this same power, for old patients of his have told me how the sun seemed to come out when he entered a sick room."

Dr. Sheahan, who died when Henry was a teenager, was a fine athlete in his younger years, and so good a baseball player that many professional clubs entertained thoughts of signing him up. Even though Henry was not a sports enthusiast, he was quite athletic, well into his adult years. He was also a good swimmer, and enjoyed sailing.

The coastal city of Quincy, located just south of Boston, was complete with tidal creeks, salt meadows and harbor islands. During Henry's youth just before the turn of the century, he and his boyhood friends could go "in 20 minutes from the brook and the muskrats to the glories of the main street and the white oilcloth tabletops of the rather solemn ice cream parlor." One of his boyhood friends was Alva Morrison of Braintree; the youngsters often picked strawberries together. Morrison eventually provided some of the photographs that would be used in Henry's classic book nearly 40 years later. He also aided Henry in donating his beloved Fo'castle to the Massachusetts Audubon Society in 1960.

Henry attended the Adams School and, later, the Adams Academy, in Quincy. At Adams Academy, headmaster William Everett greatly influenced Henry. "Superb scholar and Victorian eccentric all in one," he said of Everett. "He upheld in that forlorn school and in a commercial town an arrogant integrity of the things of the mind and a fierce belief in their importance."

The Sheahan house on School Street in Quincy, where Henry Beston grew up. The house was later torn down.
(Photo courtesy Marie Beston Sheahan)

In 1905, Henry enrolled in Harvard College in Cambridge. He graduated in 1909 with a Bachelor of Arts degree. Two years later, he earned a Masters of Arts Degree. A member of the Pi Eta fraternity, he also did some acting, was a member of the Thumb Tack Club and was on the staff of The Harvard Monthly. A former classmate recalled that "at that time, the college had prohibited the appearance of neophytes in the morning chapel because of the smell of beer, so we were taken to his (Henry's) room in Drayton Hall, where he read the Bible to us."

Another Harvard classmate was a man named Paul Turner. Turner's daughter, Anna, grew up to be known as Nan Turner Waldron, author of the book *Journey to Outermost House.*

A lifelong friendship also took shape between Henry and Theodore Roosevelt, Jr., the son of the 26th President of the United States. Roosevelt, an aspiring poet at Harvard, later became Assistant Secretary of the Navy. Writer Francis Russell recalled how Henry once told him of his visit to the White House with "Young Teddy" on holidays. One morning during a visit, Henry woke early to eat breakfast alone. Then, recalled Russell, "the president strode in, slapped him on the back, and announced heartily, 'Nothing wrong with a boy who gets up early and eats ham and eggs for breakfast!'"

After leaving Harvard, Henry spent some time in Quincy perfecting his writing craft. In 1914, he returned to Harvard as an English department assistant. Then, in 1915, Henry recalled "a pleasant August afternoon, and the Sunday papers brought along on a family picnic at the beach, and great headlines, a picture of Kaiser Wilhelm and the War. My own recollections here turn into something of an old film."

Feeling a sense of loyalty to his mother's native country, Henry used his medical knowledge as a member of the Harvard Ambulance Service with the French army "in Lorraine at the wood of the Bois le Pretre." His brother, George, a Quincy physician, also served in France in a hospital of the British Expeditionary forces.

Henry's recollections were of "a long, long winter, the great melancholy sound of distant cannon in the night, a bombarded town and the arriving whizz and rending crash of the big shells, an air shell at Verdun which all but got me." The April 22, 1916 edition of *The Patriot Ledger* of Quincy referred to the

Battle of Verdun as "the greatest battle ever fought in the history of the world."

"His service in the ambulance section, known as the Section Sanitaire Americaine, No. II took him right into the seat of the battle, where the trenches were strewn with dead and dying and where huge shells from German cannons made life continually one of the greatest hazard," stated *The Patriot Ledger*.

Already a well-known correspondent for newspapers and magazines, Henry penned the first of many books – *A Volunteer Poilu* – based on his World War I experiences. He returned home with many items from the battles -- including a gas mask, his own trench helmet and German shells and grenades. He also photographed actual warfare.

On May 3, 1916, Henry recalled his experiences for the Special Aid for American Preparedness Society of Boston. "Words fail to depict conditions they fight under," he said of the French soldiers. His address to the Society resulted in numerous pledges of support raising money for the ambulance corps.

In 1918, 30-year-old Henry became an official press representative with the U.S. Navy, and was the only American correspondent aboard an American destroyer when a submarine was engaged and sunk. He also had the unique privilege of being the only American correspondent to travel with the British Grand Fleet. These experiences were the basis of his second book, *Full Speed Ahead* – an effort that, a few years later, he begged *Boston Transcript* reporter Clarissa Lorenz not to read:

It "is nothing more than a journalistic effort much hampered by the intricacies of an oversensitive censorship – an imbecile corps which stopped me from making dangerous and surprising statements. 'Oh, you mustn't say the water is wet! The Germans might learn of it' they would protest shrilly. 'Oh, you mustn't say the sun is rising in the East, the Germans will hear of it,' and so on, ad nauseam," Henry said.

Henry took "great pride" in serving as an enlisted man attached to the submarines. "That bizarre sensation of going down deep into the sea – I felt it especially one day when buying a teapot in Ireland, then disappearing with it under water. Extraordinary! It was one glorious Jules Verne apprenticeship."

These first two books -- which Henry later labeled as "journalism" -- did not come without cost. Even though he had been presented with the American Field Service Medal in 1919, the horrific war experiences had clearly taken their toll on Henry. The time had come to close the door on this chapter of his life, and find out where another door would open.

For the next few years, Henry settled into an apartment at the Parson Capen House in Topsfield, Massachusetts, about 30 miles north of Boston. It was in Topsfield that he completed the manuscript to *A Volunteer Poilu* three years earlier.

"I only sought to know and hear as little as I could," Henry said of retreating from the war horrors. His writing turned in another direction, and Henry wrote a book of original fairy tales -- *The Firelight Fairy Book*. An edition featuring a special foreword by Colonel Theodore Roosevelt Jr. followed in 1922, and a school edition was published in 1923.

Illustrations for *The Firelight Fairy Book* were provided by Maurice "Jake" Day of Maine, who later drew Bambi for Walt Disney. The book garnered rave reviews from Abbie Farwell Brown of *The Boston Herald* on December 6, 1919 – "I am sorry for children who grew up too soon to know *The Firelight Fairy*

Book," she wrote. "These little stories are just what fairy tales should be."

Then one day in 1921 another fairy tale of sorts took shape, when Henry met a young aspiring poet Elizabeth Coatsworth.

Elizabeth and Henry were introduced one day at Elizabeth's sister's house, and the towering gentleman was immediately noticed. "He was wearing a white navy uniform which set off his height and broad shoulders, but above all, the tanned vitality of his face and fine hands," Elizabeth recalled many years later.

Elizabeth told of how the relationship came about in an interview with *Down East Magazine* in 1978. "We had a regular New England 10-year courtship," she said. Henry reportedly said he wanted to marry her right then and there.

Henry and Elizabeth became close, often dining out and attending the theater together. It wasn't long before Henry found employment in New York City, working as an editor for *The Atlantic Monthly's* newest property, *Littell's Living Age*. At the time, *The Atlantic Monthly* was transforming the publication into what Henry referred to as "a modernized magazine of international news and interests." His task was to translate information from European publications into American news. Meanwhile, Elizabeth traveled extensively in the Middle East and Europe.

Henry and Elizabeth continued writing to each other often, encouraging their respective creative efforts. In 1921, she told Henry of her interest in an Alaskan author and artist, Rockwell Kent, whose works Henry had viewed in New York.

Throughout his tenure at *The Living Age*, Henry became more and more frustrated with the editing profession. He shared his feelings in many letters, including those to his brother, George. "He was an editor, but father said he wanted more artistic freedom to write," recalls George's daugher, Marie Sheahan.

Henry Beston, second from left, aboard a naval vessel with Mary Cabot Wheelwright, far left.

(Photo courtesy Wheelwright Museum of the American Indian, Santa Fe, NM)

The final straw came for Henry after three years at *The Living Age* office.

"Then one spring morning a street piano, going off at the curb below with an explosion of notes, broke through to a disused part of my mind, and I resigned my paste pot and shears," Henry noted. "No longer would I translate the balderdash of European politicians or concern my living innards with that foul post-war world of tenth rate careerists pushing each other about on the graves of my own generation."

Since *The Firelight Fairy Book* was enjoying a successful run, Henry returned to Topsfield and wrote another collection of fairy tales called *The Starlight Wonder Book*, which was published in 1923. One of its stories, *The Wonderful Tune*, was translated into several languages overseas. Once again, illustrator Maurice Day provided many enchanting pictures for Henry's books.

The fairy tale books were also the first to be written with Henry's middle name, "Beston," which was his father's mother's surname. His two war yarns were published under his given name of Henry B. Sheahan.

Henry had always described himself as "somewhat of a wanderer," and he certainly began to fulfill that role over the next few years. The Castile region of Spain, New Mexico, Central America, Topsfield, New York City and Cape Cod were his destinations of choice.

Henry expressed a fondness for the Cape's outer beach in the early 1920s, and it wasn't long before he was out wandering with the Coast Guard patrols for a magazine article entitled *The Wardens of Cape Cod*. It was the late winter and early spring of 1923 when Henry found himself enamored with the Coast Guard officers and their work. The Coast Guard patrols walked the outer beach of Cape Cod for six mile stints each night, regardless of the weather. Even though he joined the men walking endless miles through driving rain, he referred to it as "in many ways quite the most wonderful experience I've had on land."

During those early years on Cape Cod, he was a guest of George and Mary Smith of Eastham, who served as lightkeepers at Highland Light in Truro. He fondly recalled the experience in *The Outermost House* -- at night he "would lie awake, looking out of a window to the great spokes of light revolving as solemnly as a part of the universe."

Henry spent one summer in Spain, taking "a long journey afoot from West to East across the austere, heraldic rock of Old Castile." An autumn and early winter in the Pueblo country of New Mexico, near the Rio Grande, which Henry referred to as "a true enlargement of experience," followed. The Navajo Indians helped to develop a deep sense of nature. Henry and Mary Cabot Wheelwright, a longtime friend from Boston, became friendly with Navajo medicine man Hastiin Klah. Wheelwright and Klah eventually founded the Wheelwright Museum of the American Indian in Santa Fe.

In early 1924, the War Department invited Henry to document the army's maneuvers of a mimic war in Panama. During this year, he also spent a lot of time in New York -- staying at the Allerton and then the Prince George Hotels – but he was also beginning to set up a place to stay in Eastham. The Sullivan family's cottage, across from the Salt Pond in Eastham, was a favorite spot.

Beverly (Campbell) Plante, a niece of the Smith and Sullivan families, recalls Henry painting the cottage's woodwork orange, with blue windmills adorning the wallpaper. Henry frequently joined the families for dinner at the Salt Pond house, or in the Campbells' house in North Eastham. On occasion, he would have the opportunity to read his fairy tales over the radio airwaves, prompting him to tell Cape friends to "get to a radio."

All the while, Henry's mail was being received at P.O. Box 215 in Quincy.

It was during this time period that Henry wrote *The Book of Gallant Vagabonds*. Even though most of the manuscript was written in New York, some of it was composed at the Sullivan house in Eastham. "To have had to linger in New York, writing my book in the hot July weather of those roaring streets, would have been pretty awful," Henry wrote in a letter to Frankie Sullivan, who rented the Salt Pond cottage to him. "That I was able to escape from this, to the moors of Eastham and the thunder of the cool sea, I owe to you..."

Vagabonds was what Henry called "a series of biographical studies of the wandering temperament, a history of men driven as by fury by a profound curiosity of life." The book focused on the wanderings of John Ledyard, Belzoni the monk, Edward John Trelawny, Thomas Morton of Merry-Mount, James Bruce and Arthur Rimbaud. *Vagabonds*, which was dedicated to Colonel Theodore Roosevelt Jr. and his wife, was published in 1925. The retelling of an old Navajo tale, *The Sons of Kai*, published in 1926.

In early 1925, Henry still wandered between New York's Prince George Hotel, Quincy, and Cape Cod. But, in the back of Henry's mind, he was making plans to build a small house on the remote dunes of Eastham. Literary and emotional peace of mind were not far off.

III. Latitude 41 degrees 57' 39 N. Longitude 69 degrees 57'08 W. Eastham, Mass.

Henry traveled most of the summer of 1925, but returned to the Cape and his new house on the dunes in late August. Then, "the year lengthened into autumn, the beauty and mystery of this earth and outer sea ..."

This was the start of the "year" on the outer beach, with Henry staying at the Fo'castle regularly through 1927, and returning semi-regularly in 1928. Basically, Henry took the best parts of each season from a two and half-year period from late summer of 1925 to the fall of 1927, and meshed it into one "Year of Life on the Great Beach of Cape Cod." Longtime friend George Rongner confirmed that Henry went back to Quincy "about six times" during that "year." Henry later admitted in a letter to Frankie Sullivan of Eastham in 1938 that it was "really well over a year."

The closing paragraphs of the foreword of early editions of *The Outermost House* also give a good accounting of the Fo'castle time frame: "My narrative concerns itself with the events of a twelvemonth, though I spent, on and off, a somewhat longer time upon the beach. There was a season in the spring when I had to leave the house a while."

The Overlook Inn in Eastham during the early 20ᵗʰ century. Henry Beston often stayed here when he wasn't braving the elements on the beach.

(Photo courtesy Ian and Nan Aitchison)

Whether it was a year or three years, Henry was on the beach long enough to print stationary. His return address read simply "Latitude 41 degrees 57' 39 N., Longitude 69 degrees 57' 08 W," followed by "Eastham, Mass." written in longhand.

Henry often stayed at the Overlook Inn, located on what is now Route 6 near the entrance to the Cape Cod National Seashore Visitors Center in Eastham. The Fo'castle was indeed "cozy enough to come to in winter," but it wasn't unusual for Henry to seek shelter in the secure confines of Tom and Mary Kelley's Overlook when the weather turned wild or the dreaded greenhead flies began their merciless attacks during the summer months. "Without their constant and ever-thoughtful aid, without their hospitable roof to turn to on occasion, without their friendly care for my interests ashore, it would have been perhaps impossible to remain upon the beach," Henry wrote of the Kelleys.

"They were very kind to me," Henry said many years later. "I had a very good time there."

So, just what did Henry have in mind for this house on the beach?

"I had no particular plan," he said. "I thought it would be a gorgeous place to live – with the roar of the surf and a wonderful view to the north and south. And to the east, the Gulf of Maine, you would find lobster buoys on the beach that drifted down from Matinicus Island. I had a little money. I used a handful to build the house. Everything went ahead. It developed in its own way."

Henry stayed at the Fo'castle until November of 1925, then returned to Quincy and New Mexico for the holidays. During his brief fall stay, the Cape was hit by a severe storm, and gunners and fishermen found themselves seeking shelter at Henry's house. "The Fo'castle was the Cape's Hotel Astoria that day," he told Clarissa Lorenz of *The Boston Evening Transcript*. The storm arrived quickly, "and, then, strangest of all, two magnificent eagles came flying and plunging at the lead of that cloud militia," he continued. "There was the water below, afraid, trembling, the whole world moving with a vibration that was as real as a hurrying heartbeat. The entire beach was in motion – sand, lumps, wreckage, beach grass torn by the roots – a gigantic mass hurtling south at 80 miles per hour."

By the next spring, Henry had already dedicated himself to being a "writer-naturalist," scribbling those words in French inside the cover of his notebook.

Henry told Lorenz all about his previous books, which prompted the reporter to ask why the author had never attempted to write detective tales.

"Because I cannot put beauty and interpretation into them," Henry replied. "John Farrar wants me to do a book on the dunes, but I don't know that I can cloister myself down there again for such a long time. You see, I live in mood cycles (and looked at Lorenz in apologetic appeal). I want next to do a novel – an adventure novel about the New England coast, and the sea, of course. My settings must have mystery, and only the sea can give that."

Later that year, Henry would encounter plenty of adventure. In the pages of *The Outermost House*, he wrote of the deadly sinking of the schooner *The Montclair*, which was traveling from Halifax, Nova Scotia to New York, off the coast of Orleans.

He viewed another incident in which the crew members of a distressed vessel came ashore right at the Fo'castle's doorstep. It was a late October afternoon in 1926 when Henry spotted a fire about eight miles out at sea. He assumed that his friends at the Coast Guard station would eventually get to this vessel -- a diesel-motored trawler known as *The Pioneer* out of Gloucester, Massachusetts -- and bring them ashore. The fire started in the engine room, and the fire eventually consumed the vessel before it sank.

Henry put his kerosene lamp on the table near the window, and waited until about midnight. Four Coast Guard boats, loaded with fishermen who had escaped by way of three lifeboats before the explosion, tried to make the daring landing. Henry, having witnessed similar events after submarine strikes in World War I, could barely make out the figures struggling through the surf.

Tom and Mary Kelley, owners of the Overlook Inn in Eastham, with son Burton. Mary Kelley often drove Henry Beston to get supplies in Orleans.

(Photo courtesy Merton Stevens)

That night, the north wind had driven the boats south of the Coast Guard station, and the vessels tried desperately to make landfall near Henry's Fo'castle.

While the Coast Guard men secured the dories on the beach, Henry opened the doors of his house to the 15 fishermen. He dressed their wounds to the best of his ability and served up a hot wine toddy and biscuits. The fishermen later raved about this treatment to the Coast Guard officers.

While the crew members were rescued, the loss of their ship meant a financial blow of $150,000 to its owner, Charles Pierce and Company of Gloucester.

Those Coast Guard officers, it turned out, made Henry's solitary stay more bearable. If Henry wanted to mail a letter, or needed help lugging supplies down

In a photograph taken by Henry Beston, the Rongner family stands at the front door of the Fo'castle. From left: George, Yngve and Selma Rongner.

(Photo courtesy George Rongner)

through the sand, they were there offering assistance. Likewise, Henry provided a warm fire and a cup of coffee at all hours of the night when the Coast Guard officers made their six-mile patrols.

"They are splendid men; I admire them wholeheartedly, and owe them a world of friendly services," Henry wrote in the *Harvard Alumni Bulletin*. "The Coast Guards of the Outer Cape have a hard task and their difficulties are too little appreciated. Patrolling the great beach in the thick snow and wild fury of a northeast blizzard is a job that calls for character, endurance, and courage of the finest kind."

One of the Coast Guard officers who became a close friend to Henry was Yngve Rongner, "who gave me my swordfish sword," according to *The Outermost*

House. Yngve's son, George, also developed a lifelong friendship with Henry.

"After meeting Henry Beston my life changed; he was a magnificent person and he talked so glowingly about nature and about history that I too became interested in that sort of thing," recalled George Rongner. "I think probably Henry Beston had more influence on my life as a youngster than any other single person."

Henry became sort of a "quasi uncle" to the young Rongner, but George is just as likely to label the author as his "hero." The two met in 1925, when Henry joined the elder Rongner at their home on Nauset Road for supper -- an evening that George, at seven years old, would never forget: "I was captivated when introduced, as he stepped forward, leaned towards me, extended his right hand and said, 'Hello, Georgie. I hope we will become good friends.' It was all right for this wonderful human to call me 'Georgie,' but I shuddered every time any other adult referred to me in that manner. I was enraptured with the way he spoke and with his vast experiences and knowledge."

Henry often visited the Rongner home, walking the entire four miles from the Fo'castle. A modest meal of quahog chowder or baked beans was usually on the table for supper, and "Mr. Beston," as the younger Rongner always addressed him, would sometimes sit at the piano and play by ear, a talent he shared with George's mother, Selma.

George and Selma would also walk from their house to the Coast Guard station at the beach, where they met Yngve (who was later entrusted with the key to the Fo'castle for many years) and then hike the remaining two miles down the beach to the Fo'castle. "One would think it tiring on the homeward trek, but we were so satiated with food and excellent chatter that it was actually a pleasure," George recalled.

George Rongner remembered many other moments with Henry:

■ "He often came to our home for the evening meal, and would draw sketches of the sea for me when it was just before my bedtime.

"He talked with me at great length, describing scenes of exotic places and in such terms it was like great music merely listening to his words."

■ "He encouraged me to read, and on almost every trip back to his Quincy home, he returned to Eastham with a couple of books for me. Whenever he passed our home on shopping expeditions or trips to and from Quincy, if any of us were outside he would wave enthusiastically with both hands, and look back until he was out of sight."

■ "I received my first lessons on birds from him, as he was an excellent ornithologist. He taught me how to identify the various species by their characteristics of size, coloring, wing bars, pattern of flying ..."

■ "Another of my early loves was astronomy, and Henry Beston showed me how to identify many constellations, Orion, beautiful Orion, being numero uno. Then came the planets, the brighter ones visible at various times, and he showed me how they orbited, seemingly, among the constellations. I also learned much about nature and the subtle changes that could be perceived only through close and continuous observation."

■ "So impressed was I by this remarkable person in my life it instilled a latent desire to write, a desire that came into being much later, when I was a senior in high school and was honored by the Orleans High School for my written version of *The*

Commercialization of Cape Cod." George Rongner, following in his father's footsteps, also joined the Coast Guard and became a writer himself.

Henry Beston and his "blessed pump" on the dune.

(Photo courtesy Wheelwright Museum of the American Indian, Santa Fe, NM)

Henry frequently visited the Eastham Schoolhouse, where he told stories to the children. Otto Nickerson, referred to by George Rongner as "the strict, reknown but fair principal" of the Schoolhouse, hosted the author in his classroom, where he would address the sixth, seventh and eighth grades. Today, the old Eastham Schoolhouse serves as a museum for the Eastham Historical Society.

Henry sometimes drew pictures of the sea or other elements of his surroundings, referring to his sketches as "something to amuse the ladies." Some of his drawings included a small figure with a backpack walking the beach; buying asparagus at a farm stand in Eastham; or whales walking upright with canes outside the Whalewalk Inn on Bridge Road.

Rongner wasn't the only one with fond memories of Henry. Alva Morrison Jr., son of the namesake who provided many notes on birds and the beach to Henry and also paved the way for the author to donate the Fo'castle to the Massachusetts Audubon Society in 1959, remembered him:

"He was one of my childhood heroes -- a great bear of a man with an enthusiasm for nature and its transcendental meaning that was closely in tune with my own."

Morrison fondly recalled the immediate reaction Henry had on a clear, starry evening, or arriving at the beach after a trip into town. "He would open up his arms and yell 'AAAAHHH!,'"said Morrison.

John Fish Jr., whose father was a neighbor and had provided photographs for the original editions of *The Outermost House*; and the late Burton Kelley, whose parents ran The Overlook Inn – Henry's "other" house in Eastham, also had kind words to describe

Henry. His size made a particular impact on all who met him.

"Big shoulders, very impressive," said Morrison. "Big, tall and broad-shouldered; heavy, but not fat," was Kelley's description. "He was BIG, congenial, and spoke beautiful English in a cultured manner," recalled Fish. "A gentleman of the old school," were the words used by Richard Beston Day, whose father, Maurice "Jake" Day, illustrated many of Henry's books. "Witty - - big, proud and handsome."

Burton Kelley noted that Henry had a "silly side" to him -- he liked to wear costumes, particularly sailor suits. However, costumes and the sailor suits weren't the only clothing items in Henry's wardrobe that turned heads on Cape Cod back in the 1920s. Years before it became fashionable, Henry wore Bermuda shorts during warm weather.

Beverly (Campbell) Plante, a niece of George and Mary Smith, recalls Henry living at the family's cottage across from Salt Pond for about a year before building the Fo'castle. Those Bermuda shorts were always the subject of lively conversation. "He was the first to wear Bermuda shorts, and all of the girls would giggle at him," said Plante.

As children, many of the aforementioned friends of the author would often visit the Fo'castle with their parents. On several occasions, Henry entertained his friends by playing the concertina, singing French songs with a rolling "R," recalled Morrison.

"People were always stopping by," Plante said. "He loved to have company."

Young Truesdale Fife of Reading, Massachusetts (and later Eastham) was another one of Henry's local friends. "He's a Cape Codder – he has lot of feeling for the Cape and for the history of the Cape and its people," Henry said of Fife.

The Kelley family came to know Henry quite well during his stay. Tom Kelley and Henry would signal each other using a lantern from the southeast window of the Overlook Inn, sparking off some lively conversation in town. Although Henry did admit to providing refuge to a bootlegger or two, there were a few local residents under the impression that the "Outermost Householder" ran his own bootleg business on the side.

The Kelleys also drove for Henry, who disliked using automobiles. A few times per week, either Mrs. Kelley, cabbie Helen Clark or Bud Rich met him at the Coast Guard Station and drove him to Orleans for supplies. "I'm very much indebted to Mrs. Clark, because I had no car," Henry said.

With his shopping completed, Henry rode back to the Coast Guard Station, packed his groceries into his "more green than khaki brown" English haversack, and hiked his way down the beach. In that haversack, he carefully arranged the milk, rolls and eggs. He kept his meals simple – his diet consisted of macaroni and cheese, noodles, baked beans, Indian pudding, corn bread, popovers, fruit and milk, which "kept him in excellent health," Elizabeth Coatsworth noted many years later in the book *Especially Maine*.

"Three days a week, I go ashore to get kerosene, milk and eggs, because I don't care for the lazy makeshift way we have of living out of a tin can," Henry said.

Those long strolls were always part of Henry's regular routine; in fact, he is fondly remembered by many in Eastham as a walker and wanderer.

It's been said that a one-mile hike through the sand is more like a two or three-mile walk on pavement. Henry walked through the sand to the Coast Guard Station on a regular basis. He often accompanied the men of the Coast Guard patrols on their six and seven-mile patrols of the beach. One spring day, Henry decided to take a walk from the Fo'castle to the bay side of the Cape -- seven and a half miles each way.

At the time of his "year" on the beach, Henry was nearly 40 years old. "I was six feet, one and a half inches tall, weighed 190 and was strong as a bear," he told Walter Teller of *The New York Times* several years later.

Elizabeth, Henry's wife, also discovered his passion for hiking when she began accompanying him to the Fo'castle after they were married. "I learned what a good beach walker Henry was, tireless in any kind of sand," said Mrs. Beston.

While Henry logged many a mile in Eastham, he wasn't trying to be a power walker before it was fashionable. "He was a wanderer, but he liked to stay close to home," recalled Alva Morrison Jr. "When he walked, it wasn't fast and brisk. He liked to take his time and observe."

When he wasn't busy walking, Henry sat at his desk writing in longhand. Chapters of the book began to take shape in the late winter and spring seasons of 1927. He completed the *Midwinter* chapter in March and sent it off to John Farrar, and by mid-spring, *Lanterns on the Beach* and *An Inland Stroll in Spring* were also in the mail. *The Headlong Wave* chapter, which appears as one of the early chapters in *The Outermost House*, was one of the last chapters Henry wrote while at the Fo'castle during the final days of his "year" in August of 1927.

"Of this year I made a book, calling it *The Outermost House*," Henry said of his time on the beach a few years later. "The moods of sky and outer ocean, the tides and rhythms of Nature and the year as one sees them in a great elemental place, what the mind makes of it, musing alone – these are its concerns."

After deciding that "it was time to close (my) door" in October, Henry's "year upon the beach had come full circle." A few more months of writing in his Quincy studio would follow. However, his days of "musing alone" were coming to an end.

In this photograph taken by Yngve Rongner of the Coast Guard, Henry Beston stands proudly in front of his beloved "Focastle."

(Photo courtesy George Rongner)

IV. Into the Mystic

By the time Henry completed his year on the beach, his overall picture of what life should be was coming into full focus.

"Whatever attitude to human existence you fashion for yourself, know that is valid only if it be the shadow of an attitude to Nature," he wrote in the final paragraph of *The Outermost House*. "A human life, so often likened to a spectacle upon a stage, is more justly a ritual ... Do no dishonor to the earth lest you dishonor the spirit of man."

Henry's experience on Cape Cod not only helped him find himself as a writer, but it also brought his life into perspective. "Living on the Cape has brought out in me a mystic something that shows 'surprise of life' to be quite the biggest thing," he told *Boston Transcript* reporter Clarissa Lorenz.

Henry was not a "religious" person – "he attended church only for aesthetic reasons," his wife, Elizabeth Coatsworth, said. Yet, harmony with the earth, sea and sky truly became a spiritual experience for the man who was scarred by the events of World War I.

"His lectures were filled with the sense of awe which is the essence of stirring religion," said Royal G. Davis of the Bangor Theological Seminary. "He gave us just what we needed – a feeling of cosmic mystery."

Through his experiences in the "Great War," Henry discovered that dishonor was on a rampage when it came to life in general. He became so distressed by what he had seen, he took to writing fairy tales for the next few years.

"He hated war with a vengeance, and the political world that caused such conflicts," recalled George Rongner. "'Brutal. Destructive. Innocent women and children being killed.' He frowned severely as he uttered such descriptions."

While in France, Henry witnessed grenades detonating in soldiers' hands. As he shot photographs, soldiers were dying only a short distance from him. At Verdun, "the German atrocities were probably the greatest. They launched a whole laboratory of gases into the French; and gas masks saw great service." As Francis Russell would write many years later, Henry would "live through the somber slaughters of the Marne and the Somme with extraordinary luck."

Henry came across "the oddest sight (he had) ever seen" at Bois le Pretre, as he told *The Patriot Ledger* of Quincy after his return from France: "In walking through the wood, cut and but with a little more than the trunks standing we saw an object in the tree. We investigated and found, pinned in a branch, a human heart. Someone had been blown to bits and by a strange chance the heart had found lodgment in the tree."

When the United States entered the war, Henry became a correspondent for the U.S. Navy. The nightmarish experiences didn't stop. Many years later, Henry painted a bleak picture for the Harvard alumni: "Here the eye remembers a morning after a chance night of many sinkings, seeing again the pale spring sun, and the enormous and desolately empty sea running north before the wind in billows of foam and yellowish green, running north, carrying with it long drifting miles of wreckage, shouldering up great packing cases and new planks, barrels aslope on a crest, bright tins with labels ungumming, life preservers and wavelets of scum – how strange it all was and how eloquent of the essentially tragic nature of human history, and the vast imbecilities of man."

Henry returned to Topsfield, Massachusetts after the war, eagerly looking for a change of scenery. The damage to Henry's psyche was complete. The scars would linger.

"Of the wax works at Versailles, of the bargaining elder statesmen snugged down upon their loot and scissoring the world, I only sought to know and hear as little as I could," he wrote to his Harvard classmates. "A hideous peace atop a hideous war was scarce to be borne."

While in Eastham, shadows of violence followed him. In 1928, Truesdale Fife, one of Henry's young friends from the Cape town, wrote proudly of his recent purchase of a gun. Henry wrote Fife back, lecturing him sternly about the consequences of killing for sport and the mishandling of firearms.

After World War II, the unveiling of the atomic bomb took Henry's disdain for war to a new level. While he held former President Theodore Roosevelt, a Republican, in high regard, the same thing couldn't be said for Franklin D. Roosevelt, a Democrat.

"Roosevelt was probably the most destructive man who ever lived," Henry wrote in a letter to Harry Elmer Barnes. "He left the civilized West in ruins, the entire East a chaos of bullets and murder, and our own nation facing for the first time an enemy whose attack may be mortal. And, to crown the summit of such fatal iniquity, he left us a world that can no longer be put together in terms of any moral principle."

"I find that my belief that the bombing of cities is evil no matter who does it or what its foul and specious 'justification' may be," he wrote of the U.S. bombing of Berlin in 1943. "This I find so out of fashion that it is dangerous to hold."

During the Korean War, in the conservative *Human Events*, Henry noted that pilots spoke of a bombing raid as "a perfect peach of a big fire" and sadly commented that "it is the talk of a culture which has lost its natural humanity." Hollywood's take on war also rubbed Henry the wrong way -- he walked away from a viewing of *All Quiet on the Western Front* at a Maine movie house in total disgust.

Henry's disdain for war came through time and time again, but he always held those who served in the military close to his heart. For years, he marched with the city of Quincy's Memorial Day parades with his brother, George, and his children, clad in a sailor suit. He also volunteered for the American Legion Post in Quincy.

In the *An Inland Stroll in Spring* chapter of *The Outermost House*, he noted how he turned south on to the main road "at a boulder commemorative of the men of Eastham who served in the Great War." He also spoke at Armistice Day ceremonies in Eastham in 1928.

Becoming out of tune with the earth and the increase in warlike activities were on the same parallel, according to Henry. "In a world so convenient and artificial that there is scarcely day or night, and one is bulwarked against the seasons and the year, time, so to speak, having no natural landmarks, tends to stand still," Henry wrote in the opening pages of *Northern*

Farm. "The consequence is that life and time and history become unnaturally a part of some endless and

Henry Beston dresses for the weather in New Mexico.

(Photo courtesy Wheelwright Museum of the American Indian, Santa Fe, NM)

unnatural present, and violence becomes for some the only remedy."

Years later, when told by a *New York Times* reporter that his books were gaining new readers, he replied: "The interest in nature is growing. People see it's a kind of impossible world and they have to have something else. I wish people would get on more peaceably."

Henry's fondness for the natural world around him grew while staying at a friend's house in New Mexico in 1924. Along with his time spent on the shores of Cape Cod and the coast of Maine, it was here that Henry found the most peace.

"We should have a living relationship with nature," Henry told an American Legion gathering in 1933. "Some kind of relationship between man and nature is necessary to the peace of his soul, something that the Indian has. Machinery is all right as a servant, but it is poison as a master."

Mary Cabot Wheelwright, a wealthy friend from Boston, and Hastiin Klah, a Navajo medicine man, were two friends who socialized with Henry during his stay in New Mexico. Klah and Wheelwright eventually founded the Wheelwright Museum for the American Indian in Santa Fe.

Henry spoke of his visit as "a memorable winter, a true enlargement of experience. The house was in the Pueblo Indian country, and beyond an orchard, unseen for trees but heard in the day's intervals of deeper quiet, lay the Rio Grande. Indian friends came and went, the western voices of cowboys mingled with Mexican voices beyond a gray wall, and on moonlit nights the distant yapping squeal of coyotes came to my ears as I stood listening at a window towards the hills."

During his American Legion lecture, Henry dwelt at some length of the nobility of soul and character he found in the 80-year-old medicine man, Klah. Henry and Klah became friends during this sojourn.

"Not so long ago I received a unique request from this fine old fellow," Henry recalled during the American Legion lecture, which was covered by *The Patriot Ledger* of Quincy. "Imagine my surprise when I found that he wanted sand taken from the shores of the Atlantic Ocean, with which to make medicine. I was glad to fill a grocery carton with Cape Cod sand and express it to the old man. No doubt it contained the magic that he was seeking. Later I received in return a beautiful hand-woven rug, which I understand, is also full of magic."

Henry journeyed between New Mexico and New England, making a grand impression on Cape Codders with the gifts bestowed upon him by his Native American friends. "One time he had been to Mexico or New Mexico and he had a wide belt on, wonderful looking man, quite tall, belt all set with jewels, you know -- red, green," one of the local women said during a recent Eastham Historical Society gathering. "The Indians had made it for him."

The Indians bestowed Henry with other gifts. One Indian chief gave him a silver and turquoise ring, with three large turquoise stones, in gratitude for kindness to the chief's son. Henry was buried wearing this ring. Later, when Henry moved to Maine, traveling Indians always had a place to stay at Chimney Farm.

Henry talked about the Indians of Cape Cod frequently with young George Rongner. Henry told Rongner all about the Nausets of Eastham, the Pamets of the Truro area and "other semi-individual tribes."

"He could spot an arrowhead when only a small portion was visible," Rongner recalled. "I remember my father picking up pieces of flint, and Henry could always tell which had been worked by the Indians."

The Indians' philosophy and Henry's soon became the same, both believing that city dwellers of modern America failed to appreciate the four seasons of the year. Henry emphatically quoted an old Indian medicine man from the lower St. Lawrence: "The whites have never made peace with the earth and it does not like them."

"Let no one without a profound religious sense venture to trespass among these Indian peoples!," he wrote of his experience with the Indians in New Mexico. "Still in poetic relation to the earth and the moods and ways of nature, they face in us a culture by nature atheistical and a people who are not priests of the earth but its destroying exploiters and enemies."

Because of that destructive nature, he reasoned that man was paying a heavy price.

"People are cheating themselves with their sophistication and blase -- like the boy who steals a march on the family the night before Christmas so there's no surprise for him the next morning," he reasoned in 1926. "That's it. We are a cigarette-smoking race. We are shutting out pictures with tobacco smoke."

Henry came to believe that wonder and mystery were the keys to life. "A world without wonder, and a way of mind without wonder, becomes a world without imagination, and without imagination man is a poor and stunted creature," he wrote in *Northern Farm*. "Religion, poetry, and all the arts have their sources in the upwelling of wonder and surprise. Let us thank God that so much will forever remain out of reach, safe from our inquiry, inviolate forever from our touch."

Marie Beston Sheahan remembers her uncle often quoting Shakespeare: "There are more things in heaven and earth, Horatio, than are dreamt of in your philosophy."

"Henry was not a theologian, not apart; with some mystics the way to reach God / spirit is to separate from the lives of others, disconnect," wrote Nan Turner Waldron in her notes for her book *Journey to Outermost House*. "With Henry there is a 'getting in touch with,' learning to be more human and activating the senses. It is OK to be human, and a part of nature, and life and death are all right.

"It was not aesthetic separation – meditation but not remoteness. Henry was never down on the natural world, nor was he pessimistic or caustic about our modern misuse of the environment. It is an 'up' sermon. It is a kindly lead, showing where we 'fit' as humans and how we do benefit from the connection with the earth."

Henry Beston's writing desk in the Fo'castle is pictured in this photograph by Nan Turner Waldron.

(Photo courtesy Butterfly and Wheel Publishing)

V. Writing 101 with Professor Beston

When it came to the qualifications of being a good wordsmith, Henry Beston had few rules.

According to his niece, Marie Sheahan, "He thought a good writer was someone who could make you turn a page."

There was no question that Henry had an oceanful of qualifications for mentoring writers. When he wasn't busy writing, he also taught at Harvard, the University of Lyons in France, and Dartmouth College in New Hampshire at various stages of his life.

Besides the vastness of experience and various accolades to his credit, there was something even more important that Henry was able to convey -- how writing was part of him and his passion for the craft.

"Nature and writing were synonymous with him," recalled Alva Morrison Jr., whose father provided Henry with many notes and photographs of birds and the beach for *The Outermost House.* "He always encouraged me to write."

Morrison remembers Henry becoming more passionate when the conversation's subject turned to writing. He would emphasize putting one's heart into the subject, gesturing with his fist.

Henry didn't fabricate his material, according to his niece. "He didn't take artistic license with the truth," she recalled. "He felt that it had to be authentic, or he wouldn't go with it."

"I didn't put in any fake stuff," Henry said in 1966. "I told everything truly."

"With his *House* and a few other books of integrity, Beston enjoys precisely the career any artist would choose," summarized Winfield Townley Scott in his book *Exiles and Fabrications*. "He has written only what he has wanted to write and as he has wished to write it, and he has fetched a durable audience. Such ripeness is for the artist really all."

While many authors turned out books at an assembly line rate, Henry was meticulous and careful with his craft. "He never struggled with anything except his writing," said his wife, writer Elizabeth Coatsworth, in a 1978 interview. She also noted that her husband liked to write at the kitchen table, as he did at the Fo'castle, and would often spend an entire morning on a single sentence. Sheets of paper would end up on the floor. "He'd sit there making popcorn balls and tossing them over his shoulder," she recalled.

Perhaps Clarissa Lorenz of *The Boston Evening Transcript* stated it best when she wrote "his originality is endless. But the French in him dictates, and a masterly control in the shaping of his work is his reward for patience."

Henry kept a strict schedule when it came to his writing. "I wrote every morning from 9 to 12," he recalled in 1966.

When asked what the tools of his trade were during a 1926 interview with Lorenz, Henry had a long list:

"First, an incredible quantity of ruled paper. Second, a large coffee mug -- blue for choice -- full of sharpened Faber No. 2 pencils (Tarkington insists on forests of pencils. Here the fountain pen is heresy). Third, at least five cubes of art gum. Fourth, an Oxford dictionary -- that concise one of Fowler's. Fifth, an old Roget's Thesaurus (easily had at ancient, second-hand book stores. Never get one published later than the 70s). But all in all, the ground-floor requirements for style are one Roget and one good ear."

Once the tools were set up in the proper order, Henry then explained how he found story ideas.

"My stories begin in various ways. Sometimes with a plot, sometimes with a picture, sometimes with a person. After I get my idea, I run away with it into a corner where I brood over it like a child with a beloved toy."

With all that in place, a story takes shape -- in a style that demands swift rhythm:

"I like the rhythmic quality of English prose. Sentences ought to follow each other like waves of the sea, and be as individual as waves. A sentence ought to come in at a fair speed, rise, break and then withdraw, leaving a free space for its successor. Now, there's only one way to get this essence of rhythm, and that's by reading and cherishing the King James text. Truly, it is my Fidus Achates and guide, invaluable in its simplicity and directness."

Henry would not rely on modern technology or gadgets, but did concede that typewriters and other such equipment were necessary for periodicals to publish on a regular basis. However, he didn't keep a typewriter on his desk.

"I have always stressed rhythm. For that reason, I could never use a typewriter. It would be fatal. Just say now, you want to start your story with a 'once upon a time a fine young fisherman rose early in the morning – 'Do you get the swing? Well then, follow along. Did I attempt to write it on a clackety typewriter, those jarring, discordant notes of the machine would run counter to the rhythm which in my sentence gets me throbbing. Why, the old noise-maker would ruin me with its 'click-click-click-click-click-kling! Whizz-z-z-z, click-click-click-click click-kling! Whizz-z-z ... It's like trying to paint a Sargent with a pneumatic paint brush."

Henry traveled all over the world during his lifetime, but his frequency for turning out books once every few years was not a high rate for most authors. "Only when he became part of the landscape could he write about it," his wife said.

Prior to settling on the Cape for that eventful "year," Henry was a volunteer for the ambulance service in France and a Navy correspondent aboard a U.S. submarine in World War I; he wrote two books that he labeled as "journalism." In between, he worked as a correspondent for magazines like *The Atlantic Monthly*, *The World's Work*, *The North American Review*, *The Bookman*, *The Mentor*, and *Ladies' Home Journal*. Books of fairy tales followed, helping to clear the horrors of war from his head. After his 40th birthday came the publishing of the book that would be his crowning achievement – *The Outermost House*.

"I know no more details of his life than that he then wrote a number of charming fairy stories and still did not manage to come to terms with himself as a writer," wrote Francis Russell in *The Country Journal*. "Only with the sea approach to *The Outermost House* did he finally find his theme."

Henry Beston and friend stand at the entrance to the Overlook Inn in Eastham in June 1928, only a few months before *The Outermost House* was published.

(Photo courtesy Merton Stevens)

Henry was critical of the writing quality of fairy tales in the 1920's – "mamby-pamby things," he said. Years later, Henry commented to Francis Russell -- "the present day crop of books – he spoke so disparagingly of the trend in writing," Russell said.

While Henry made his share of friends in Eastham during his stay here during the 1920s, there were also those who regarded the Quincy writer as a bit quirky and eccentric.

One of those who may have put Henry in the latter category was Sea Captain Robert Sparrow of Eastham.

Donald Sparrow, the captain's nephew, still has an original edition (published by Doubleday, Doran and Company) of *The Outermost House*, and in the pages of that book can be found a few comments inscribed by the sea captain in the *Lanterns on the Beach* chapter.

On page 128, Henry writes "From Monomoy Point to Race Point in Provincetown -- full fifty miles -- twelve coast guard stations watch the beach and the shipping day and night." The first comment from the captain is written here, stating that "stations do not watch."

Further down the page, Henry goes on to write of how "every night in the year, when darkness has fallen on the Cape and the sombre thunder of ocean is heard in the pitch pines and the moors, lights are seen to be moving along these fifty miles of sand." The captain writes "day of" and points it in between "every night," and then comments "What of nights when the ocean is not heard in the pines?"

On the following page, Henry writes "When the nights are full of wind and rain, loneliness and the thunder of the sea, these lights along the surf have a quality of romance and beauty that is Elizabethan, that is beyond all stain of present time."

The captain seemed puzzled by this one. "Stain?" is what he wrote next to this paragraph.

Captain Sparrow is featured prominently in the book *Growing Up On Cape Cod* by longtime Eastham resident Donald Sparrow.

Two books are consistently the top sellers at the book stores of the Cape Cod National Seashore visitor centers in Eastham and Provincetown -- *The Outermost House* and Henry David Thoreau's *Cape Cod*.

Thoreau may be the better-known author of the two, but Henry's book is often compared to Thoreau's classic. This pairing did not sit well with the second Henry. "He never liked to have *The Outermost House* compared to *Cape Cod*," noted Elizabeth. "'Thoreau had very little heart,' he would say."

The mere mention of *Cape Cod* and *The Outermost House* in the same sentence troubled Henry. His views about Thoreau and "*Cape Cod*" rang loud and clear in a 1950 letter to Donald Trayser of Barnstable, the author of the 1951 book *Eastham, Massachusetts: 1651 to 1951*. Henry had just written the introduction to the newest edition of Thoreau's book, but told Trayser that *Cape Cod* had "always seemed to me a very dull book." Then, in rather bold fashion, he continued, "However, I did my best for 'the other Henry!'"

The Outermost House has been called the *Walden* of Cape Cod literature, referring to what is perhaps Thoreau's best-known work. Unlike *Cape Cod*, which was written after several long walks on the Outer Beach of the Cape, *The Outermost House* followed the same theme as *Walden* -- a year of life in a setting of seclusion. While Henry was not a Thoreau fan, it's quite unlikely that he could have written *The Outermost House* without the presence of *Walden*.

Thoreau, whose *Cape Cod* was published following his death in 1861, and Henry, who saw *The Outermost House* roll off the presses in 1928, shared some common traits. Both were born in Massachusetts. Both spent extensive periods of time on Cape Cod and later in Maine and Canada. Both authors did not use their given names in their work. Both were graduates of Harvard. Both had French blood flowing through their veins. Both took musical instruments (Thoreau a flute, Beston an accordion) to the houses that would become their spiritual cocoons.

The similarities ended there. While the name of Thoreau often comes up in conversations about Beston, the author of *The Outermost House* never saw himself on the same page and would acknowledge that when asked if he was influenced by the Civil Disobedient of Concord.

"No, I think not," Henry told *The New York Times* in an interview a few years before his death. "I admire Thoreau but don't care much for him. He wasn't warm enough."

Henry's perceived lack of warmth and heart on Thoreau's part was evident in this correspondence to Winfield Townley Scott:

"I suppose that I do link up with Thoreau, but I do not read him and have not been under his influence," Henry said. "He is not a naturalist. What interests him and stirs him most deeply are the principles governing the individual life when that life is enclosed in a gregarious society. If I tie with anybody, it is with Richard Jefferies. We are both of us scholars with a poetic joy in the visible world."

Jefferies was a 19th century English nature writer who also expressed a love of solitude and walking. His influence on Beston resonates in the closing passages of *The Outermost House*. In Jefferies' *The Story of My Heart*, he writes "instinctive worship of sun and earth and sea, the same mystic adoration of the human form as the supreme embodiment of all natural beauty."

Henry referred to himself as "sometimes as vague as a Dunsany figure in the mist," referring to Irish poet Lord Dunsany, author of *The Book of Wonder* and many essays and plays. It is believed Henry attended some of those plays in Boston. The sketches in Dunsany's work were very similar to those of illustrator Maurice Day, who collaborated with Henry on his fairy tale books.

Henry's favorite books that he took to the Foc'astle – "Shakespeare's plays, the Bible, W.H. Hudson and Longfellow, whose poems of rain and sea have always appealed to me." Also, Forbush's three-volume *Birds of Massachusetts*. Sherlock Holmes stories and *Rubaiyat* – "a great favorite." According to friend George Rongner, Henry was not fond of the work of mystery writer Mary Roberts Rhinehart.

Henry was also close friends with John Farrar, editor of The Bookman during the 1920s, and Harvard essayist / poet, David McCord. Farrar was also an organizer of the Bread Loaf Writers' Conferences at Middlebury College in Vermont; faculty members and speakers for the conferences included McCord, Scott and poet Robert Frost, who participated in the organization of the Beston / Outermost House tribute committee in 1964. Frost and T.S. Elliot, a contemporary of Henry's during his years at Harvard College, were the only writers other than Henry to be awarded the Emerson / Thoreau Medal by the American Academy of Arts and Sciences.

This photograph by Nan Turner Waldron shows the kitchen of the Fo'castle.

(Photo courtesy Butterfly & Wheel Publishing)

VI. *Welcome to the Fo'castle*

Henry Beston's book, *The Outermost House*, has captivated generations since it was first published in 1928, but many of the literary classic's readers might think twice about actually staying in the 20x16-foot house on the dunes of Eastham.

"A generous use of windows on every side of this miniature roof-tree enabled its sole occupant to miss nothing in his pleasant task of recording the great pageant of the seasons where the salt winds blow," were the enchanting words used by Arthur Wilson Tarbull in his 1932 book, *Cape Cod Ahoy!*, describing Henry's Fo'castle. "An old hatch from a wreck for a doorstep, a bottle or two for candlesticks, a diminutive brick fireplace for 'a household god and a friend,' a pump that never failed, food in a full locker, and a few good books on a shelf hardby -- these were his snug and shipshape companions."

The Fo'castle had two rooms – a small bedroom and a larger living room / kitchen. Over the doorway was the "swordfish sword" given to the author by Yngve Rongner of the Coast Guard, and in the living room was his writing desk. "How I loved that place, and how I loved sitting in the same chairs and writing at the same desk as he had, before," George Rongner fondly recalled.

"I spent many nights in the Outermost House as a child - a glowing refuge in the Atlantic storm and a wonderland of moonlight when camped in summer at dune top," said Alva Morrison Jr., whose father was a lifelong friend of Henry's. "There is no better sleep than a night caressed solely by the lackadaisical slap of half tide."

However, life in the Fo'castle was not easy, and no one knew that better than Nan Turner Waldron, who stayed at the Eastham beach house from 1960 to 1978 at various intervals, actually logging more time there than Henry. Waldron wrote the book *Journey to Outermost House* chronicling her experiences there.

The house was not a typical dwelling, even for the beach. Seven shuttered windows in the main room offered a panoramic view in three directions. The shutters protected the windows from bad weather, but Henry often closed them on bright sunny days, due to the glare that was too much for him.

The consistent roar of the surf was always heard, often shaking the house with each crashing wave.

"It was a lonely life out there," Henry told *The New York Times* in 1966. "Nobody patted me on the back, but the life had great appeal. The most solitary time was on certain wild nights. Sometimes I would be inside when a single wave would crash on the beach and shake the whole house. I always had a fire going – kept fire on the hearth. I was an old-fashioned person – always liked a hearth fire. I had a teacher who used to say hearth fire was the only fire fit for a human."

"The Outermost House was not your usual vacation rental," Waldron recalled in October 2000, shortly before her death. "Except for a three-burner gas plate and a gas refrigerator (which occasionally worked), it was a remnant of a bygone era -- no electricity, no radio, no running water and no car."

The Fo'castle, located two miles south of the Coast Guard station, was situated in a prime location for fishing, birding or just wandering on the outer beach. However, before there was time for any of those activities, there were daily chores to be done:

■ PRIME THE PUMP: Henry's "Blessed Pump" may have "never failed or indulged in nerves" in the Fo'castle's early days, when it was located outdoors on the dune. In later years, after the Fo'castle was moved twice and the pump installed inside, it produced salty tasting water and often malfunctioned. Filling a pail and the tea kettle with clean fresh water was required, and that was after "pumping until the water ran fresh," Waldron noted. Those staying at the house brought jugs of their own drinking water, as high tides would occasionally turn the water brackish.

■ FILL THE WOOD: Henry's old fireplace was eventually replaced by a wood stove, but wood still needed to be gathered and ashes cleaned out. As any year-round camper knows, fire is a necessary heating element during a good portion of the year. "I never allowed myself a fire in cold weather until I had replenished a good supply for the whole day," Waldron said.

Finding wood on the beach, so easy to do in Henry's day, became more and more difficult as beach buggy traffic increased. "Fishermen began driving to the marsh to the inlet when the bass were running -- no one walked any more," Waldron said. "One night I counted 44 buggies. They picked up the best wood that the sea had to offer."

"I had an enormous pile of wood in back of the house," Henry said of his stay many years earlier. "And I gladly would have had more if I could have got it."

■ GARBAGE AND WASTE REMOVAL: An area was designated for burial out on the dunes for what was probably the most difficult of the regular chores. "There was no bathroom, just the addition on the east side of the house with space for storage and an indoor 'outhouse,' and then you had to empty the bucket, usually in a hole dug out on the dunes," Waldron recalled. "Henry never mentioned an outhouse, although I suspect there had been one."

■ LAMP MAINTENANCE: The chimney's two kerosene lamps always needed cleaning and the wicks had to be trimmed daily, unless a candle or flashlight was used.

■ STORM MAINTENANCE: When the weather turned rough, more chores were required. High winds meant covering everything in the little bedroom. "The ceiling of the room was open to the rafters -- unlike the main room, and the wind drove the fine sand under the shingles. You could hear it gently sifting into everything, which meant that the covers had to be carefully shaken out before and after a night's sleep."

Richard Shanor chronicled his experiences while staying at the house for *The New York Times* in August of 1964. Shanor noted that "washing was kept to a minimum." Dishes were dunked and left to dry in the sun, and the amount of clothes worn and washed was also a small number. Basic washing was done outside in an enamel basin.

"After a day or two, swimming in the icy waters of the North Atlantic made us feel clean enough not to miss showers and other bathroom amenities -- or almost," he concluded.

Shanor wrote that while staying at the house, days had no set schedule. "Dinner was at sunset -- around a fire in the dooryard or in the kitchen sitting room of the house. Both places had a view of the marsh and the sun going down behind it."

Anyone easily bothered by insects probably wouldn't have enjoyed a stay at the Fo'castle. Henry himself avoided the house for extended lengths during the summer, and even mumbled some less than pleasant things about the greenhead flies on the road to the Fo'castle's dedication ceremony in 1964. The insects, that crowded the entry to the house, provided food for the birds in the area.

"The birds were never afraid of me, and when the weather was bad, they took shelter near the house," Henry wrote in a 1963 letter to Waldron.

"I could be on the porch or inside and still be birding with a yellow-breasted chat policing the entry where the flies were plentiful, warblers searching the corners of the porch, sparrows flitting from grass to bush, a harrier sweeping past the windows ... the house was a bird blind supreme," said Waldron.

The Fo'castle was also a place where a sense of humor was a prerequisite for admission.

"The pump balked, the refrigerator failed on the south wind if the door were open, the milk soured, the bread molded, the firewood got wet, and the public could treat you as a curiosity," Waldron recalled.

Shanor concluded that this is what life was like before electricity. "There was the exhilaration of living in the clean air of the dunes, with the sound of the ocean on one side, the marsh and its busy life on the other, and the birds everywhere."

Bill and Peg Whittlesey of Western Massachusetts stayed at the Fo'castle on several occasions in the early 1960s. They were particularly impressed by the early sunrises. "When you stand up on top of the dune, at 4:30 say, the world is dark," Peg

Whittlesey told *The Boston Globe*. "Then, it all lights up slowly. Other places, you see a patch of light. But here, you see the whole world light up."

In the summer of 1962, Helen Finlayson chronicled her experiences staying at the Fo'castle for the *Massachusetts Audubon Magazine*: "To enjoy and understand Nauset barrier beach, one should live in the Outermost House and venture out at any time, day or night, to contemplate the plants, the animals, the sea, the land, and the sky, which surround its remoteness. It is in such a place that one begins to be aware of the basic forces and the great rhythms of the world and of the enormous pressure of life itself."

VII. Weathering the Storms

"Creation is here and now," wrote Henry. Nothing did more to destroy – and create – the landscape of Henry's beloved beach than the constant pounding of Atlantic storms, or "nor'easters," as they're called in this part of the country, on the shores of Cape Cod.

The Fo'castle faced one of its earliest durability tests during the famous storm of February 19-20, 1927, which Henry described in the *Midwinter* chapter of *The Outermost House*. The storm, highlighted by a near full moon tide and relentless sleet, sent the surf cutting through the dunes and into the marsh, leaving the Fo'castle "no longer looking down upon the sea, but directly into it and just over it," Henry wrote. "The Fo'castle stood like a house built out into the surf on a mound of sand."

Newspapers categorized the 1927 storm as the worst since the "Portland Gale" of 1898. Inland, highways were buried under drifts of snow, but a wild mix of precipitation fell on the coastal areas. On the open sea, many vessels were beached or sunk, as was the case of the CG-238 boat that Henry wrote of.

As Henry noted in his book, the boat, plagued by engine trouble, was anchored off the outer beach of Truro and Provincetown. The Associated Press reported that the boat, caught up in wind gusts of 75 miles per hour, was just a few hundred yards off shore, and that its lights were visible to Coast Guard officers on the beach. A steamer came into view, "giving momentary hope to the anxious watchers on shore," according to the report.

The officers tried to signal the steamer, but to no avail, and the vessel was soon consumed by the ocean. The doomed vessel's blinking lights were in view of the Coast Guard officers at the High Head Tower in Truro, who relayed the distress signal to Coast Guard headquarters in East Boston. A rescue mission consisting of two destroyers was immediately dispatched, but didn't arrive in time. The CG-238 was smashed to pieces on a sand bar.

Watchers at the High Head Tower reported that a high tide was expected at about 3 a.m. that morning, and signaled to the boat to weigh anchor in the hope that the tide might carry the boat over the outer bars and on to the beach. "If the tide had done this, the men, in all probability, would have been saved," the Associated Press reported.

Premonition may have played a factor for two crew members. One member escaped the ship's fate because he was bedridden with illness and never made the trip. The ship's newly-promoted captain, Jesse Rivenback, reportedly told a friend that he didn't feel right about making the trip on the one-year-old vessel, and had asked that his body be sent back to his native North Carolina if anything happened.

Henry's words, "Creation is here and now," rang true over and over again during the Fo'castle's 53 years. Countless storms and billowing surf pounded Coast Guard Beach. "Every time one of those billows hit poor old Cape Cod, poor old Cape Cod went back several feet," Henry wrote in 1933.

Henry described a storm that "was not an easterly at all; it was a mid-ocean moved in against the Cape" in January 1933. The storm started on a Friday night, with 20 feet of dune between the house and the water. The following morning, just five feet remained, with a noon high tide still to come. The water came to within a foot of the door before subsiding. At the close of the storm, three feet separated the house and the breakers. "The O.H. came through, Old Father Ocean mercifully saving me once again," Henry noted.

Unfortunately, the water had come close enough. "As three feet of sand does not offer enough leeway of protection, I am now having the house moved back. Work has already begun," he wrote in a letter to the editor of *The Patriot Ledger* of Quincy, Massachusetts. The letter was printed on February 7, 1933 (ironically, 45 years to the day before the Blizzard of 1978).

"It might be that the house had served its purpose and its hour," Henry wrote in a lengthy article for *The New Bedford* (Massachusetts) *Standard Times* on March 19, 1933. "But its hour had not come and The Outermost House is still monarch of its sand dunes on the outer beach."

The storm began on a Thursday afternoon as drizzle. Easterly winds picked up in intensity the following day and Henry decided to check with his Eastham friends on the well-being of his little house. He called the Overlook Inn and spoke with his longtime friend, Tom Kelley. The Overlook Innkeeper took the short drive down to the Coast Guard Station (Nauset Station had no public telephone). Kelley talked with Kenneth Young, who reported that the house was probably safe for the night, despite the wind and heavy rain.

The next morning, when Henry awoke, readings on his household barometer continued to drop, and the water levels in Hingham Harbor were also disturbing. At 9 a.m., Henry and an unnamed friend left for Eastham, encountering an unstable mixed bag of precipitation along Route 3. On the Cape, conditions became worse, but Henry was able to spot his house through the storm when he reached the Eastham windmill.

A "Cape Cod snow of fine particles" fell as Henry arrived at the Coast Guard Station, where he found only a few feet remained between his house and the edge of the cliff. Henry, however, decided to look for himself, despite the warnings that the sea could break through the barrier beach into the marsh.

Henry and his friend walked the top of the dunes toward the house, waiting for the waves and torrents to shallow out enough allowing them to run across one of the cuts and the face of the next wave. "The sight of those four Niagara torrents in the heart of the stormy dunes remains an unforgettable picture," he noted.

When the two arrived, they discovered four feet of frontage remaining, with a 12-foot drop to the sand and ocean below – quite a difference from when Henry last left the house in December. He entered the house and started gathering books, keepsakes, a telescope and other items, placing them into a bag and then handing it to his friend outside the window. He pondered the situation, wondering if it would all be there the next morning or scattered about on the beach and in the sea.

Only a few feet separate the Fo'castle from the edge of the cliff following the 1933 storm.

(Photo courtesy Eastham Historical Society)

Henry and his friend trudged back to the Coast Guard Station, noting that a change in the wind to the northwest might save the house. Henry worried through the night at the Overlook, despite the assurances from Tom and Mary Kelley. The next morning, the house endured, and Henry celebrated by having a cup of coffee in the company of the Coast Guard men.

Following the storm, the move took the house further back on the dune. Later on, other weathering hollowed the dunes under the structure which led to another relocation of the house in 1944. Had it not been moved at that point, the house would have collapsed into the ever-widening hole in the dunes. With this move, Henry replaced the fireplace with a new chimney and wood stove. The house was no longer on a dune top, but down in the hollow of the dunes.

The Fo'castle's new location, now facing Fort Hill instead of the outer beach, may have kept it safe from the elements for another 34 years. This however, apparently did not jibe with Mrs. Beston. "What had been the cock-of-the-dune became a pathetic little heath hen," Mrs. Beston told Nan Turner Waldron, author of *Journey to Outermost House*, a few years after Henry's death.

Even with its new location, the Fo'castle remained on borrowed time. In January 1948, a storm with high winds tilted the house a couple of feet toward the north. Following a 1966 storm, Colonel Eugene Clark and Sam Bartlett of Eastham visited the Fo'castle to see if the ocean water had reached the house. Indeed it had – in fact, this was becoming a larger concern with every weather event.

Storms and surf continued, reducing the dunes and overall land mass of Nauset Spit over the next 12 years. Waldron was staying at the house before and after a severe storm in May of 1977, where the water paid another call on the Fo'castle's doorstep. She noted that storm, complete with high winds and 20-foot waves, tore six new gaps in the dunes.

"Creation is here and now."

"The phrase had been the soul of the book, rooted in this house," Henry concluded. The 1933 storm, he continued, was "but a renewal. If it went in the gale, it would go tragically but honorably, knowing no neglect and suffering no wounds of age."

VIII. Another Door Opens

Although he had not completely closed the door on his Cape Cod experiences, Henry returned to Quincy, spending less and less time at the Fo'castle. He rented a studio at the Cliveden Building on Hancock Street (known today as Hancock Plaza) in Quincy.

Henry moved back into his family's house on School Street, and spent a lot of time wandering around Quincy's downtown area. Henry always had a sweet tooth, and often visited the local bakery for eclairs. He pestered his brother, George, to be a little more lenient with his niece (George's daughter), Marie. "When can that child have some candy?!" Marie Sheahan, known as "Mimi" to family members, recalled her uncle questioning her father. Henry brought his nieces to the theater – "he liked Shakespeare a lot," Marie recalled.

Henry frequented the Crane Memorial Library in the downtown area, and the offices of *The Patriot Ledger* newspaper. Walter Emerson, the paper's assistant editor and theater critic, befriended the author, and the two men talked for hours about literature and the theater, whether it was at the Ledger office or at Emerson's residence at the local YMCA.

While the middle chapters of *The Outermost House* were written at the desk of his Cape Cod retreat, the first two and final chapters weren't composed until late in 1927 and early 1928. Finally, on April 2, just after 9 a.m., the final manuscript was complete.

The Outermost House was published on October 5, 1928.

Though not a smashing best-seller at first, *The Outermost House* received many favorable reviews, including a lengthy and positive commentary from Emerson in the pages of *The Patriot Ledger*. Within a few months, several hundred copies of the book were sold in the local store in Eastham. However, the most notable accolades probably came from John Riddell of *Vanity Fair*. *The Patriot Ledger* proudly trumpeted Riddell's critique of the hometown author's work:

"I genuinely believe that Henry Beston is one of the few great prose writers in this country today.

"This high tribute to a writer whom Quincy is proud to call her own is paid by John Riddell in a review of Mr. Beston's latest book, *The Outermost House*, in the December number of *Vanity Fair*.

"*The Outermost House*, he continues, "is strong medicine. I genuinely believe that it will live for other generations. It stands alone, not only in this publishing year, but in any year."

This unstinted praise is heightened by the fact that Mr. Riddell is noted for the severity of his judgments. His praise is praise indeed. His full comment on Beston's book follows: "This is no more a book than the sea is a book; than the days and months are chapters in a narrative of the year."

When the book was first published, Henry was told by fellow writer Corey Ford that successful sales and establishment of the book would take time. By 1929, Henry traveled to London, where *The Outermost House* was about to go through a press run for a British edition. While in London, he gave some thought to writing a book about the cloud formations of England, but never developed the idea further.

By 1929, the success of *The Outermost House* wasn't the only part of Henry's life that was taking off. His longtime relationship with poet / writer Elizabeth Coatsworth, had reached the point where Henry proposed marriage in January of that year. Coatsworth accepted, and the couple was married at the home of her sister, Margaret Smith, in Hingham, Massachusetts on June 18, 1929. George Sheahan served as best man for his brother, and Margaret Smith served as matron of honor for her sister. Mabel Davison, who had moved to New York after living in Paris during World War I, Mary Cabot Wheelwright of Boston and four other couples attended the nuptials.

Coatsworth, who was perhaps best known for her Newbery Medal winning children's tale *The Cat Who Went to Heaven*, was a statuesque woman, only two or three inches shorter than Henry. It was publicly announced that the couple would take a motorcoach tour of the east coast following the wedding, but they quietly escaped to Eastham for a short stay at the Fo'castle. Henry leaked that information to his young friend Truesdale Fife of Eastham, but asked him to keep the secret.

Henry stopped to visit his friends in the lower Cape area to introduce Elizabeth. While at the Rongner household he was met with some resistance. Henry's marriage to Elizabeth apparently didn't sit well with young George Rongner. "I was hostile to her when he came to our home to introduce his bride, for after all, there now was a wedge between us, and in my childish thoughts I did not wish to share him," Rongner recalled.

Though the Bestons made frequent visits to the Cape, their use of the Fo'castle began to decline. They frequently stayed at the Overlook Inn, but later on they stayed at a house on Hemenway Landing overlooking Nauset Marsh and John Smart's cottage on Great Pond, located just off of what is now Samoset Road. While staying here, the Bestons ate their meals at the nearby Overlook Inn.

While at the Smarts' cabin, Henry entertained thoughts of writing a book about the inland Cape, actually writing a few chapters, but never completing the manuscript. He managed a chapter about eeling at Salt Pond, and began another on the marshes of the area. He also asked friends, particularly Fife, for information on animal life that lived in and around the kettle ponds of Eastham.

By this time, *The Outermost House* had been through three printings. Henry signed a contract with the publisher and entertained notions about another Eastham book for a few more months -- but it was never to be. Henry was sure that *The Outermost House* was destined to be a classic, and didn't want to diminish it with another Eastham effort. Before it was ever completed, the fledgling manuscript was torn up.

In 1930, the Bestons' first child, Margaret, was born, and another daugher, Catherine, followed in 1932. Margaret's first Christmas was spent with her father at the Whalewalk Inn on Bridge Road in Eastham. Henry actually gave some thought to purchasing the Whalewalk Inn from owner Richard Kent before being turned off by the price.

While the purchase of the Whalewalk never occurred, the acquisition of the land surrounding the Fo'castle did. Henry leased the land when he built the house. On March 5, 1932, the property was officially transferred to Henry from Edna Nickerson Hurd.

Henry also spent time visiting friends in Maine during this period of his life. Maurice "Jake" Day of Damariscotta, Maine was one he saw often. Day, the illustrator for Henry's fairy tale books, told him about a farm for sale in nearby Nobleboro, Maine.

Henry jumped at the chance to buy it. "It sounds fine," his wife said after he proposed the idea over a fish and chips lunch in a Quincy restaurant.

The hectic pace of suburban life in Hingham was not to Henry's liking. Traffic was increasing, and the nearby ocean, abutting Boston Harbor, was becoming more polluted.

Henry needed to tune in to his environment in order to write about it, and even though there were some nearby attractions that were near and dear to his heart (the Blue Hills in Milton, the herring run in Weymouth and the salt marshes of Quincy, among others), it was now time for a change in location.

The Bestons traveled frequently between Hingham and Maine while taking long trips to Mexico and Europe.

Henry didn't write another book until 1935, when he published *Herbs and the Earth*. This endeavor was based on his experiences and observations in his herb garden while living in his new farmhouse, "Chimney Farm."

The Bestons wintered in Hingham and summered in Maine. Cape Cod trips were less frequent, unless the Fo'castle needed maintenance or moving. The little house was broken into and ransacked in 1937, prompting Henry to pay "Junior" Campbell of Eastham to keep an eye on it.

Following *Herbs and the Earth*, Henry's historical collection, *American Memory*, was published in 1937. Extensive Canadian travel followed, and Henry wrote *The St. Lawrence* for the *Rivers of America* series in 1942. Alva Morrison Jr. remembered Henry wanting to write about the Rio Grande for that series, but the publisher turned him down.

Meanwhile, *The Outermost House* enjoyed continued success. With its ninth printing, the book was published by Editions for the Armed Services, a non-profit organization which made pocket-sized books exclusively available for members of the Armed Services.

In 1944, the Bestons moved to Nobleboro permanently, and Henry settled down to write *Northern Farm*, chronicling his life as a Maine farmer (1948). *Northern Farm* was written in the same fashion as *The Outermost House*, with the focus on the cycle of the natural year. To this day, many refer to it as "The Outermost Farm."

In *Northern Farm*, Henry emphasized that a return to understanding nature was vital to human existence. The farmhouse was heated by a central fireplace, and lacked many modern conveniences. The Bestons drove a car and owned a telephone, but Henry preferred not to use them if at all possible. Noted *Christian Science Monitor* columnist and author John Gould and his wife, Dottie, were friends of the Bestons. "After breakfast he tied a necktie around the telephone so he couldn't hear it ring and he wouldn't answer it all day," recalled Dottie Gould.

John Gould, who wrote *The House that Jacob Built*, and Dottie were living in a log cabin at Lisbon Falls, Maine in the 1940s, prior to building the house that became the subject for Gould's book.

Henry Beston overlooking his land at Chimney Farm in Nobleboro, Maine.

(Photo courtesy Wheelwright Museum of the American Indian, Santa Fe, NM)

"Henry called one day and wanted to 'come and break bread' with us," said Dottie. "He came by train and I went down to the station to get him. He was a huge man and I am a little one, and he scared the daylights out of me. However, we broke bread and had a nice visit with him."

Henry also kept busy writing for periodicals. In 1947, as a columnist for *The Progressive*, a liberal periodical founded by Senator Robert M. LaFollette, Henry penned (or in his case, "pencilled") the column *Country Chronicle*. Many of those columns became part of *Northern Farm*.

White Pine and Blue Water, a collection of Maine nature writing that Henry compiled and edited, was published in 1950, followed by *Henry Beston's Fairy Tales*, a collection from his earlier books, in 1952. Henry frequently lectured on the subject of nature writing at Dartmouth College in New Hampshire.

During his later years, Henry told Francis Russell that he might want to write his memoirs one day, but that never materialized.

Henry had become a noted author with his efforts, but *The Outermost House* remained his biggest accomplishment. In 1948, a French translation of *The Outermost House*, was published under the title *Une Maison au Bout du Monde (A House at the End of the World)*, much to Henry's delight.

Back on Cape Cod, owners of an abutting gunning camp had eyes for the property where Henry had written his masterpiece two decades earlier. Fiske Rollins and Bill Farnham made overtures about purchasing the Fo'castle and its land from Henry. He declined, but Rollins and Farnham still kept their hopes alive of someday owning that land.

By this time, Henry was celebrating his 60th birthday, and with age came fewer trips to the Cape. Other writers, such as Sylvia Plath and Ted Hughes, became temporary residents of the Fo'castle.

Throughout the 1950s, Henry gathered many honors. Both Dartmouth and Bowdoin Colleges presented him with honorary doctorates. In 1951, Henry wrote the introduction for Barnstable author Donald Trayser's Eastham Tercentenary publication. In 1959, the American Academy of Arts and Sciences presented Henry with the Emerson-Thoreau Medal for distinguished achievement in the field of literature. This honor's only other recipients were T.S. Eliot, a contemporary of Henry's at Harvard, and Robert Frost. Henry was also named as an honorary editor for

National Audubon Magazine. His greatest honor of all came in 1964, when a special ceremony dedicating the Fo'castle as a National Literary Landmark was held on Henry's beach in Eastham.

Sadly, with high honors came ill health. Henry, who always had trouble with his blood pressure, was eventually confined to a wheelchair due to the complications of this disease. In 1959, with help from his longtime friend, Alva Morrison, an ailing Henry, no longer able to care for his Cape Cod spiritual haven, donated the Fo'castle and the surrounding land to the Massachusetts Audubon Society. As Henry wanted it, the Audubon Society rented the Fo'castle to birders and solitude seekers as long as the house stood on the beach.

In 1963, Colonel Eugene Clark of the U.S. Coast Guard and a friend of the Beston family, ventured from his Sandwich residence to meet with Henry's Cape Cod friends. Many of these friends, who had not seen or spoken with Henry in over 30 years, were told of Henry's health problems. Clark took tape recorded messages from Harvey Moore, Yngve Rongner and Kenneth Young to the Beston farm in Maine, much to Henry's delight.

In 1965, the Fo'castle had exterior refurbishing, and miniature versions of the house were made. One such miniature was sent to Henry in Maine. He reportedly kept it next to his bed and often held it in his hands.

While the one-time vagabond could no longer get up and wander about at his leisure, many journalists and admirers would write or telephone him (when it wasn't being muffled by a necktie). One admirer, 41-year-old Nan Turner Waldron, had made the first of many trips to the Fo'castle only two years earlier. Waldron penned the book *Journey to Outermost House* nearly three decades later about her own experiences in the dunes of Nauset. She often sent beach plum jam to the Bestons.

In a letter dated September 16, 1963, Henry related his love of the setting that would go on to deeply affect this mother of four children from Sharon, Massachusetts. "Your letter brings the sense of the Great Beach back very vividly, and it makes me happy to think that people who feel the beauty as you do still shelter under the Fo'castle's roof," Henry wrote to Waldron.

Over the next few years, many paid what would be their final respects to Henry. A few months before his death on April 15, 1968, George Rongner visited with the author at Chimney Farm. Rongner, who followed his father, Yngve, into the Coast Guard, was en route from Boston to Southwest Harbor, Maine. While passing through the area, he decided to telephone the Bestons in advance, hoping to stop in for a visit. Elizabeth met him outside upon his arrival. "Henry is not well and is confined to a wheel chair," she said.

Rongner then recalls being "ushered inside. Henry, seated at the table, smiled broadly, and stretched out his arms."

"Georgie, old-timer," Henry said. "What a thrill. So good to see you. Come here and let me hug you."

"Feeble as he was, he held me in a bear hug for so long Elizabeth asked him to release me so I could have dessert," Rongner said.

Yngve Rongner, left, and George Rongner pose in this photograph taken by Colonel Eugene Clark in 1962.

(Photo courtesy George Rongner)

Henry showed him some of his keepsakes and a couple of paintings. A glass of wine and a toast to George's parents, Yngve and Selma, followed.

During the conversation, Henry looked at him, "smiling broadly all the while, and occasionally reaching over to pat my hand," Rongner said. Then came "another long lingering hug as we bade one another farewell."

Rongner had endured many experiences in his life – he served in World War II and for over two decades with the Coast Guard. However, his last day with Henry is one that will remain in his heart forever.

"My eyes become moist whenever my thoughts drift back to that final meeting with my hero."

IX. The Coronation

In the May 5, 1974 edition of *The Worcester Telegram & Gazette*, literary editor Ivan Sandrof reflected on what Cape Cod means to those who live there – "an impression I shall never forget."

"Vividly I see it in a sunburst of emotion," Sandrof wrote. "It took place 10 years ago on October 11, 1964."

The events of that day meant an awful lot to Henry Beston. It was on this unusually warm Sunday afternoon that nearly 2,000 people attended a special ceremony at Eastham's Coast Guard Beach to honor the author and dedicate the site of *The Outermost House* as a national literary landmark.

At the age of 76 and in frail health, Henry traveled to Eastham one last time for the ceremony. In addressing the crowd of admirers, he read from the final paragraphs of his classic book.

Sandrof, who was the chairman of the dedication committee for this event, stayed intent on Henry's words. A few moments later, he realized that something special was happening.

"Dozens of people were weeping," Sandrof noted. "Beston's soaring words had reached their hearts and emotions. These were true Cape Codders. They knew the Cape, and they cared ..."

Henry Beston, left, talks with Toni Peabody, wife of Massachusetts Governor Endicott Peabody, inside the Fo'castle during the dedication ceremony on Oct. 11, 1964.

(Photo courtesy Eastham Historical Society)

Henry, who had been living with ill health for some time, would live another three and a half years after that day. The event, referred to as "The Coronation" by the Bestons, was truly a special day in his life.

"Then in 1964 came the final honor at the very moment when it could give him most happiness, for even by the next year he could not have gone to Cape Cod, nor spoken publicly," recalled his wife, Elizabeth Coatsworth. "But the honor came in time, so that he lived his final years knowing that his work had been truly recognized."

The dedication first took shape in late summer of 1964, when Massachusetts Governor Endicott Peabody and his wife, Toni, along with Sandrof and

Secretary of the Interior Stewart Udall, began the task of putting together a major event in a short amount of time. It was Toni Peabody who first proposed the idea to Udall in late August. By September 24, press releases were sent out to media outlets, announcing the event that would take place on October 11. The governor's office sent invitations to selected guests. *The Cape Codder* newspaper took out a full-page house advertisement in its issue prior to the event, saluting Henry and his book.

The Bestons drove from Maine the day before the event, staying with relatives on the South Shore before heading on to the Cape. The big day began with a special luncheon at the Nauset Inn in Orleans, with the public ceremony at Coast Guard Beach set for 2 p.m.

Governor Peabody presided as chairman, with Superintendent of the Cape Cod National Seashore Robert Gibbs, Allen Morgan of the Massachusetts Audubon Society and George Palmer of the National Park Service speaking. Governor Peabody then presented a dedication plaque and a picture of the State House to Henry. The Reverend Daniel Weck of the Universalist Church of Eastham gave the invocation and benediction.

Governor Peabody compared Henry's writing style to the King James version of the Bible with its rhythmic cadences of words in his search for harmony between man and the universe.

"We are here today partly because you have given the American people a heightened awareness of the Outer Beach as part of our way of life," the governor said. "You described the great beach and the ocean which comes in up on it, as no one else ever could or ever will.

"*The Outermost House* as a testament has had immeasurable influence."

Henry, clad in a brown tweed coat and a black basque cap, began speaking in a feeble voice, but gained strength as he went on. Standing behind a microphone and leaning on his cane, he urged the crowd to "touch the earth, love the earth, honor the earth -- her plains, her valleys, her hills and her seas."

"I thank all the eminent men and women who have honored me with their presence today," Henry said. "We are all in one joy in knowing that the great beach where we stand has been set aside by our government. You have honored human awareness that perceives the nature about us and attempts to find words to give another kind of harmony, human, as well as that of the elements."

Among those in attendance that day was an aspiring young author named Robert Finch, who would later pen the introduction to the newer editions of *The Outermost House* and write many Cape Cod nature books of his own. "It was the first and only time I ever saw Henry Beston," Finch has fondly recalled on several occasions.

Eastham Selectmen Maurice Wiley and Luther Smith were on hand, along with Fo'castle carpenter Harvey Moore and Dartmouth College graphics professor Ray Nash and his wife, Hope. Hope Nash designed the jacket cover for Henry's book from a wood carving.

Guests and others in attendance then climbed into beach buggies for the two-mile ride to Henry's "Fo'castle," which he donated to the Massachusetts

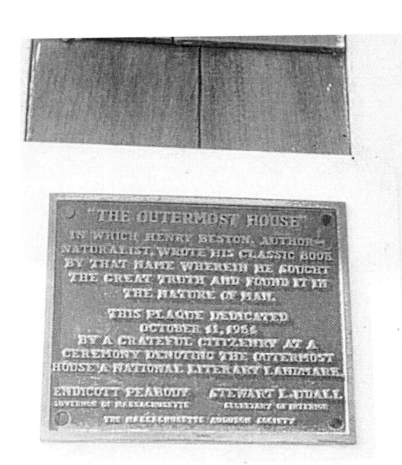

The plaque dedicating the Fo'castle as a National Literary Landmark.

(Photo courtesy Thornton W. Burgess Society, Sandwich, Mass.)

Audubon Society only a few years earlier. Many more set out on foot, taking the marsh road that Henry himself had walked so many times before.

Lines formed at the little house, and guests managed to all get a view of how Henry had lived during that famous "Year of Life on the Outer Beach" nearly four decades earlier. "All these people will never fit in the house," a small child said.

A dedication plaque was presented to Henry that day, but the Fo'castle went without one until January 4, 1965, when Mrs. Peabody and her son, Endicott Jr., along with Gibbs and Morgan, dedicated it at the house in 20-degree temperatures. The ceremony had been postponed from December 22, 1964, due to high tides flooding the area around the house.

"It's a pleasure to know that the Fo'castle still lives in people's hearts, which is even better than being a national literary monument," Elizabeth Beston wrote in a November 1964 letter to Nan Turner Waldron. "The 'occasion' was so filled with enveloping kindness that it left Henry very happy."

Henry's health continued to deteriorate over the next few years. Confined to a wheelchair and frustrated over not being able to wander about, bouts with pneumonia and gout became common, and the man who was a towering strength of wisdom to so many finally succumbed to his own ill health on April 15, 1968.

The creator of the legacy of *The Outermost House* was gone. Nine years, three months, and 27 days later, the magical setting for it all would be next.

X. The Blizzard of '78

At 5 a.m. on the morning of Tuesday, February 7, 1978, radio newsman Bob Seay of WVLC in Orleans, Massachusetts started his day with a phone call to the local police dispatcher. A mighty winter storm was raging over Cape Cod and the rest of eastern Massachusetts since the day before, and this would no doubt be the day's lead story.

"Oh, my God!" the dispatcher exclaimed in Seay's ear. "You should see Coast Guard Beach. There's nothing left!"

"I couldn't *imagine* it," recalled Seay.

This was a news flash that longtime Eastham residents had anticipated for years. Seay got into his car and drove down to the beach to observe it for himself.

"There were six or seven homes along there, mostly shacks, and The Outermost House," Seay described the barrier beach that protects Nauset Marsh in Eastham. "I was absolutely shocked -- to look out and see the entire Coast Guard Beach area totally over washed. The parking lot was essentially gone, and all the houses were floating around or dismantled. You could see quite a few of them in Nauset Marsh."

The Outermost House, the 20x16-foot beach dwelling that author Henry Beston dubbed the Fo'castle in 1925, was swept off its wooden foundation during the night. So many times before, Henry's house had survived the ferocious nor'easters, narrowly escaping the ocean's rage. Just two weeks earlier, a storm of similar strength hit the area, but the beach escaped significant damage due to low tides.

This time, Nauset would not be so lucky. The earlier storm did leave one mark -- the off-shore sandbars were obliterated, leaving it vulnerable to significant damage if another dangerous storm came this way.

Now, it was here.

The "Blizzard of '78," as it's come to be known throughout New England and other northeastern U.S. states, is perhaps best known for the tremendous snow totals in that area. *USA Today* classified it as an "honorable mention" on its list of "The 20th Century's Top Ten Weather Events."

The National Weather Service forecast in the morning newspapers, which included the Cape Cod region, for Monday, February 6, 1978, stated: "Snow heavy at times tonight. Probable accumulations of eight to 16 inches. Windy with drifting. Snow ending tomorrow. Low tonight in the teens. High tomorrow in the 20s. Northeast winds 25 to 40 mph tonight and north winds 25 to 35 mph tomorrow."

This storm caused blizzard conditions from New England to Philadelphia, with over 27 inches falling in Boston and as much as four feet over Stoughton, Massachusetts and Woonsocket, Rhode Island. Fifty-four people died in the storm -- many were stranded in their vehicles on Route 128 around Boston, where hundreds of cars and trucks were trapped for a week. The storm caused over $1 billion in damage.

The Fo'castle in its final location near Nauset Marsh. Incoming tides threatened the house many times until it was finally consumed by the ocean in February of 1978.

(Photo courtesy William Quinn Sr.)

Along the coast, Henry's house and the surrounding dunes were just the beginning of the casualties. The storm's effects led to nine additional houses being lost to the sea in nearby Chatham. The winds decimated 340 houses and damaged another 6,000 along the coast. The five-man crew of a Gloucester pilot boat, a five year-old girl and 62 year-old man from Scituate, Massachusetts were among the casualties of the ocean's waves. The sea hurled boulders, lobsters and sand into oceanside streets and residences.

On Monday at midnight, a high tide on a new moon, together with the storm surge waves, drove the tide to 14.5 feet above mean low water. "It really wasn't a blizzard on the Cape; it was a *tidal* event," Seay emphasized. "It was this *huge tide* -- four feet above normal. It wasn't so much those huge waves, but the ocean level itself was high."

Oddly enough, the preceding Sunday was a quiet, tranquil day. "Something's wrong," Nan Turner Waldron, author of the book *Journey to Outermost House*, said repeatedly that day as she led a bird walk in Sharon, Massachusetts. Not one bird could be heard or seen.

"We were down there (at Coast Guard Beach) the Sunday before and there was no hint," Eastham's Conrad Nobili said. "It was a beautiful day and it was strangely quiet." Nobili also lost his Coast Guard Beach house to the storm.

While Cape Codders were sensing something not quite right with the quiet conditions, meteorologists along the East Coast were frantically checking weather conditions across their half of the country. A large Arctic high pressure system covered the area from the Midwest to New England, causing sub-zero morning low temperatures near Boston the week before. A small low-level storm was making its way from central Canada to Pennsylvania, but its meeting with a cold high-level disturbance caused a secondary low pressure area to form off the coast of Virginia. This storm quickly intensified and moved northward, but ran smack into the cold high pressure area, which had centered itself over northern New England. The storm stalled off the New England coast, and with the intense battle zone developing around the system, heavy precipitation and high winds resulted. Heavy bands of snow developed just a few miles inland, but across Cape Cod, the Blizzard of '78 left little, if any, snow.

In this photograph taken by Marilyn Schofield of Eastham, the Fo'castle floats sideways in Nauset Marsh before being carried out to sea, where it was crushed in the waves.

(Photo courtesy Eastham Historical Society)

"It was a rainstorm, and a *fierce* rainstorm," Seay said. I was struggling to get home the night before. The wind was wailing. I had heard that the wind indicator at the Chatham Coast Guard Station had blown off -- they claimed that it hit 120 miles per hour, but that was never really verified." The official high wind speed was clocked at 92 miles per hour, 18 mph over hurricane force.

The wind proved itself the major culprit behind the damage in this weather event. The strong gales drove what was already an astronomically high tide into overdrive.

"What was most dramatic was to see the ocean actually come across that parking area and actually cut off the rest of the Coast Guard Spit," Seay said. "So I got back in my car, went back to the Visitors Center on Route 6 and called in a report from a payphone: 'I've just been at Coast Guard Beach and all the houses have been swept away,' and within a few minutes, I could start to see cars coming down."

Cape Codders began heading to the beaches -- storm watching at the beach is a favorite activity of Cape Cod residents during every season. Of course, the elements can also be quite intimidating.

"The water was just coming in and it was so scary," recalled longtime Eastham resident Marcia Nickerson. "It was horrendous; I just couldn't believe my eyes. It was awesome and at the same time frightening -- all I could think of was that there was nothing that could stop it."

Another Cape Codder viewing the sea's destruction was William Quinn, author of several books about Cape Cod shipwrecks and a cameraman for ABC News. Quinn's trip to Coast Guard Beach, where he ventured with his camera to shoot film for ABC, began a three-day adventure that took him up close with the waves in Eastham and through the high snow drifts outside Boston. "I remember a crowd of about 300 or 400 people at Coast Guard Beach, who were there because of the surf," said Quinn, who had visited Henry's Fo'castle earlier in his career. "The waves were coming over the dunes and tearing the beach apart." Towering dunes were reduced to low sand mounds; the waves rolled over the barrier beach, pushing it westward.

Quinn jumped into his jeep and headed north toward Boston, but encountered snow in Plymouth. He hooked up with a Boston policeman driving in to work, but "we were stopped by 12-foot drifts just before Mattapan," Quinn recalled. Quinn managed to get his film to a Howard Johnson's motel, where it was picked up by the local ABC affiliate, WCVB-TV. The next day, ABC hired a four-wheel drive vehicle and a helicopter so that Quinn could shoot footage of the storm's destruction in other areas off the Massachusetts coast.

Back in Eastham, longtime resident Marilyn Schofield was near Hemenway Landing, camera in hand. Schofield is a great-granddaughter of Coast Guard Captain Abbott Walker, who once advised Henry 53 years earlier that his house's original location was too close to the high tide line.

On that fateful day, the Fo'castle was floating in Nauset Marsh. Schofield snapped a picture of the house floating sideways, half-submerged in the icy water. "The house was heading southeast -- going out," Schofield recalled, adding that it was caught up near Fort Hill for a while until another high tide took it out into the ocean. The ocean crushed the small house just off Nauset Heights in Orleans.

The Coast Guard Beach bath house and parking lot were completely destroyed. Twenty-four years later, pieces of the parking lot asphalt continue to turn up in the Coast Guard Beach sands. The force of the waves also unearthed a 50-foot long concrete septic tank near the bath house.

This storm was the worst to hit the Cape in years, immediately prompting comparisons to the Portland Gale of 1898 and the storm that Henry wrote of in 1927. Then, on Tuesday (February 7), as the next high tide rolled in just after 11 a.m., the eye of the storm parted the clouds over Eastham.

Though the wind was still blowing, it subsided somewhat. The sun shone bright, causing temperatures to climb into the high 40s. "There were crowds on the Coast Guard Station hill -- people were out there with picnics," Schofield recalled. "At the same time we were experiencing sunshine and temperatures in the 40s, it was snowing like crazy in Boston and Providence," Seay marveled. "I couldn't believe it."

As the hurricane's eye was passing over the area, aerial photographer Dick Kelsey of Chatham undertook an unbelievable task. The eye of the storm was approximately 40 miles in diameter, and with the maelstrom moving at about eight miles per hour, Kelsey had between two and three hours to fly over the Nauset area, take his pictures, and return to Chatham. One of his photographs captured the Fo'castle breaking up in the waves.

As the storm moved north and away from Cape Cod, the ocean receded and the winds died down. Fragments of the Fo'castle turned up in different places. Orleans resident Mark Holland and Nan Turner Waldron recovered a window (with one pane intact) and several shingles on Nauset Beach in Orleans. Authorities eventually removed the larger splintered fragments of the house from the beach, fearing a safety hazard.

On the Eastham side, Bill and Trudy Craig, who traveled from their home in Sudbury, Massachusetts, walked down toward the end of the spit. "Boards from the Outermost House were coming up on the beach," Trudy Craig recalled. "The park rangers told us they were wide boards from the front or the side, but were definitely pieces of the house." Bill Craig added, "We saw the platform of a shell, almost like a deck of a cottage."

Conrad Nobili was among those to find a piece of the Fo'castle. In a photograph at the Eastham Historical Society's Schoolhouse Museum, Nobili is pictured holding the piece of the Fo'castle where the National Literary Landmark plaque, affixed to the structure just 13 years earlier, was still in place. That section, as well as two chairs from the Fo'castle, were given to Eastham natural resources officer Henry Lind and taken to the Massachusetts Audubon Society's Wellfleet Bay Sanctuary.

Nobili's beach house, which he had stayed in since coming to Cape Cod from Milton, Massachusetts in the early 1950s, was also a victim of the storm. It was located about 500 yards north of the Fo'castle.

"I designed my house to be moved -- ready to move in a month or so," Nobili said. "I figured if I got by the spring tides in February, I'd be OK."

In the pages of *The Outermost House*, Henry wrote about Eastham residents flocking to the beach the day after the great 1927 storm, piling up timber that washed ashore and surveying the conditions. Cape Codders arrived in throngs again in 1978; in fact, so many people came to Coast Guard Beach during the week after the Blizzard, that Eastham and Cape Cod National Seashore officials designated Doane Road and Ocean View Drive as one-way to traffic. *The Cape Cod Times* reported a total of 3,264 cars traveled to the Coast Guard Beach entrance.

The 32 acres of Henry's property, stretching nearly 350 feet on both the ocean and marsh sides upon donation to the Massachusetts Audubon Society in 1960, was covered by the ocean. Should natural forces ever restore the sand, the Massachusetts Audubon Society can reportedly claim it as theirs.

Wallace Bailey holds up a piece of the Fo'castle following the 1978 blizzard. Note that the National Literary Landmark dedication plaque is still attached.

(Photo courtesy Eastham Historical Society)

Rebuilding Henry's Fo'castle on the beach was discussed, but quickly dismissed. The Massachusetts Audubon Society saw such a move equal to "playing Russian roulette with the sea, a dangerous game."

The houses were lost to the sea, and many expected that Coast Guard Beach was lost as well. "Everybody thought that was it -- the beach had been destroyed," Seay said. "I'll never forget when Seashore Superintendent Lawrence Hadley held his press conference and said, 'Oh, there'll be a beach -- next summer, there'll be a beach. Don't worry.' It was hard to believe, but in fact, that's when we all started learning about westward migration of the dune system. Yeah, there'll be a beach -- everything is just moved back."

To many who read about and experienced *The Outermost House*, the Fo'castle's demise was sad, but expected.

"It was hard to visualize the damage that day, but it didn't hit home to me personally until I made the drive down to Coast Guard Beach about three days after the storm," recalled Bruce Richter, who was stationed in Boston with the Coast Guard. Years earlier, Richter spent many summers surfing near the Fo'castle. "Looking at the devastation, I really felt that I had lost a friend."

"I think Henry would have said a great storm was the way it should go," said Elizabeth Coatsworth Beston following the '78 storm. "He was never afraid of change. His *Outermost House* is forever young in his book, as he would have wished."

In a news story announcing the demise of the Fo'castle in *The Boston Herald-American*, Christine L. Kane wrote, "But in the place of the landmark itself, New Englanders are left with the modest legend of a man who sought solitude among natural forces that exist 'above and beyond the violences of men.'"

"*The Outermost House* marked the place where one man searched for and found his humanity in nature," wrote Wellfleet Bay Sanctuary Director Wallace Bailey in the April 1978 edition of the Massachusetts Audubon Newsletter. "That place itself has now returned to nature. We can best commemorate both man and place by continuing the search."

**Today, a tribute plaque to Henry Beston and *The Outermost House*
overlooks the Atlantic Ocean at Coast Guard Beach in Eastham, directly
in front of the Coast Guard Station.**

(Photo by Don Wilding)

XI. The Legacy of the Dunes

Nearly 11 years following the publication of Henry Beston's *The Outermost House*, a photograph of the Fo'castle appeared in the August 17, 1939 edition of *The Boston Herald*.

"Although it has *no historical significance*, many pilgrims trek the two miles over sand to visit the place where Beston worked," the caption read.

"*No historical significance ...*"

Twenty-two years later, almost to the day, the "place where Beston worked" had played a large factor in the establishment of a new national park – the Cape Cod National Seashore – which extended from the tip of the Cape at Provincetown, Massachusetts down to the elbow of the peninsula at Chatham, Massachusetts. Forty years following the establishment of this land being set aside for preservation by President John F. Kennedy, Henry's words continued to be emphatically quoted by United States Representative William Delahunt of Massachusetts at a special anniversary celebration at the Cape Cod National Seashore Headquarters in Eastham.

"*No historical significance ...,*" indeed.

Since it was first published in October of 1928, *The Outermost House* has undergone dozens of printings. At the Cape Cod National Seashore's book stores, *The Outermost House* and Henry David

Thoreau's *Cape Cod* are the top sellers. Rachel Carson, author of the ground-breaking *Silent Spring*, said Henry's book was the only book to ever influence her writing.

"Beston was a conservationalist and environmentalist ahead of his time," according to writer Francis Russell.

The book was published in 1928. Henry Beston died in 1968. The house was consumed by the massive February blizzard of 1978. Yet, today, the "Gallant Vagabond's" message still endures.

"I suppose there are millions who wouldn't know what Beston is talking about, but obviously there are a good many people who do know," wrote Winfield Townley Scott in his book *Exiles and Fabrications*. "And I think they know it in the sense of discovery, in the sense of apprehending – as readers so often find when they come upon a significant poem – that here is something they feel but could not define."

It was no wonder that Henry's wife, Elizabeth Coatsworth, referred to him as "a great opener of windows." Cape Cod has a strong lure to it, with many people from all walks of life yearning to smell the salt air, sense the pounding of the surf and hear the cries of the gulls, no matter what the season. Henry opened those windows for readers everywhere.

"To read *The Outermost House* is to gain new respect for Cape Cod," wrote Yolande Murphy in the October 12, 1964 edition of *The Attleboro Sun* of Attleboro, Massachusetts. "To the ornithologist, it is a veritable encyclopedia; to the biographer, a treasure trove of Cape Cod lore; to the seafarer, a great adventure story; to the poet, a masterpiece of candance; to the anti-preservers, a profound warning of the dire consequences."

"For many persons, 'Outermost House' has been the beginning of a new world of insight," wrote Jane Harriman on October 4, 1964 in *The Boston Sunday Globe*. "Now considered a literary classic on a level with the works of Thoreau, this slim volume first published in October 1928 has introduced Cape Cod to countless readers, and more than that, it has shown them a beauty and peace."

"*The Outermost House* is an inside story of individual perception – experience written in a manner befitting the man," according to Walter Teller of *The New York Times*. "Henry Beston believes he wrote 'rather an English style.' Be that as it may, one finds in his book dignity, courage and a point of view."

Literary critic Walter Emerson of *The Patriot Ledger* newspaper of Quincy, Massachusetts, a longtime friend of Henry, perhaps summed it up best when he wrote "If you want to know him, read *The Outermost House*.

"In it he himself is revealed, his great love for untarnished nature, his ever-inquiring mind so filled with the beauty and mystery of his carefully recorded observations, his very religion and philosophy, all are there. And Henry is, indeed, worth knowing."

Credits

Cover photo of Henry Beston and sketch of Beston walking the beach provided by Beverly Plante.

Cover photo enhancement: Tami Harris

Photographs provided by:

The Eastham Historical Society, Eastham, Mass.

The Thornton W. Burgess Society, Sandwich, Mass.

Nan Turner Waldron / Butterfly & Wheel Publishing

Merton Stevens

Wheelwright Museum of the American Indian, Santa Fe, NM

George Rongner

Ian and Nan Aitchison

Personal Interviews by Don Wilding

Bob Seay

George Rongner

John Fish Jr.

Alva Morrison Jr.

Nan Turner Waldron

Merton Stevens

Beverly Plante

Marie Sheahan

Donald Sparrow

Conrad Nobili

Marilyn Schofield

William Quinn Sr.

Bill and Trudy Craig

Marcia Nickerson

Personal Interviews by Jon March

Dottie Gould

Information provided by:

Ted and Nan Waldron / Butterfly & Wheel Publishing

The Eastham Historical Society, Eastham, Mass.

The Thornton W. Burgess Society, Sandwich, Mass.

The Patriot Ledger, Quincy, Mass. (1916 – 1978)

The Quincy Historical Society, Quincy, Mass.

The Crane Public Library, Quincy, Mass.

Beston Family Papers, Special Collections and Archives, Bowdoin College Library, Brunswick, Maine

Fran Murphy Zauhar / St. Vincent's College, Latrobe, Penn.

North Dakota Quarterly / University of North Dakota, Grand Forks, ND

The American Academy of Arts and Sciences, Boston, Mass.

George A. Smathers Libraries, Special Collections, University of Florida

Cape Cod stirs Caper's heart, Ivan Sandrof, Worcester Sunday Telegram, May 5, 1974

The Junior Book of Authors, edited by Stanley J. Kunitz and Howard Haycraft, The H.W. Wilson Company, New York, 1934.

Letter from Rolfe family to Nan Turner Waldron, July 31, 1965

Letter from Henry and Elizabeth Beston to Nan Turner Waldron, Sept. 16, 1963

Thornton W. Burgess Society – Col. Eugene Clark interview with Elizabeth Beston, 1963

A Volunteer Poilu, Houghton-Mifflin, 1916

Full Speed Ahead, Doubleday & Doran, 1919

The Book of Gallant Vagabonds, Doubleday & Doran, 1925

Francis Russell, *The Outermost Man*, *The Country Journal*, March 1976

Clarissa M. Lorenz, *Boston Evening Transcript*, 1926

Clarissa M. Lorenz, *Atlantic Monthly*, Oct. 1978

Especially Maine, E.C. Beston, Steven Greene Press, Brattleboro, Vt., 1970

Twentieth Century Authors, Edited by Kunitz and Haycraft, H.W. Wilson Co., NY

New York Times Book Review, by Walter Teller, 1966

Harvard Class of '09 newsletter

Letters from Henry Beston to Francis Sullivan, 1924 and 1937

Bangor Theological Seminary Alumni Bulletin, 1950

Northern Farm, Doubleday & Doran, New York, by Henry Beston

The Outermost House, by Henry Beston, Doubleday & Doran, New York, 1928

The Outermost House, by Henry Beston (Henry Holt & Co.)

Journey to Outermost House, by Nan Turner Waldron, Butterfly & Wheel Publishing, Bethlehem, CT, 1991

Down East Magazine, March 1978, "Tea with Elizabeth Coatsworth"